THINK AGAIN LOOP

How to Rewire Your Brain, Build Real Wealth,

and Stop Falling for the Same Old Nonsense

KEN KONET, M.Ed., MBA & IBRAHIM ROBLE

Humbolton Press

Copyright

THINK AGAIN LOOP: How to Rewire Your Brain, Build Real Wealth, and Stop Falling for the Same Old Nonsense

Published by Humbolton Press, Florida.

ISBN: 978-1-966703-39-6

First Edition: 2026

Cover design by Humbolton Press Interior layout by Humbolton Press

10 9 8 7 6 5 4 3 2 1

Printed in the United States of America.

Disclaimer

This book is intended to provide general information and commentary on the subjects covered. It is not intended as a substitute for professional financial, legal, tax, medical, or psychological advice. The authors and publisher disclaim any liability arising directly or indirectly from the use of, or reliance on, any information contained in this book. Individual financial circumstances vary, and readers are strongly encouraged to consult qualified, licensed professionals before acting on any information presented here. The authors are not licensed financial advisors, certified public accountants, attorneys, or licensed mental health professionals. Anecdotes and case studies have been altered, composited, or attributed to representative individuals; resemblance to specific living persons is coincidental unless explicitly noted.

A Note on Sources, Commentary, and Fair Use

Think Again Loop is a work of original commentary, criticism, and educational synthesis. It engages substantively with Napoleon Hill's *Think and Grow Rich* (1937) as the structural and historical predecessor of the framework offered in this book. The authors gratefully acknowledge Hill's enduring contribution to the literature of personal achievement and have endeavored to honor that contribution by preserving the integrity of his original thirteen principles while updating their explanations to reflect contemporary research in neuroscience, cognitive psychology, and behavioral economics. This book is a transformative work intended to extend, modernize, and respectfully critique Hill's framework, not to reproduce or replace it. Readers are warmly encouraged to read the original *Think and Grow Rich* alongside this volume.

The authors further acknowledge with respect and gratitude the published work of the following authors and researchers, whose ideas and findings are referenced, paraphrased, and discussed throughout this book under the principles of fair use, scholarly commentary, and educational citation: James Allen (*As a Man Thinketh*); Albert Bandura; Daniel Kahneman (*Thinking, Fast and Slow*); Charlie Munger (*Poor Charlie's Almanack*); Norman Doidge (*The Brain That Changes Itself*); Anna Lembke (*Dopamine Nation*); T. Harv Eker (*Secrets of the Millionaire Mind*); Vicki Robin and Joe Dominguez (*Your Money or Your Life*); Robert Kiyosaki (*Cashflow Quadrant*); MJ DeMarco (*The Millionaire Fastlane*); Morgan Housel (*The Psychology of Money, Same as Ever*); Annie Duke (*Quit, Thinking in Bets*); Gabriele Oettingen (WOOP / Mental Contrasting research); Gary Klein (Pre-Mortem methodology); Steven Levitt (*Freakonomics*); John Ratey (*Spark*); Wallace Wattles (*The Science of Getting Rich*); Jen Sincero (*You Are a Badass*); Tim Ferriss (Fear-Setting); Tristan Harris (Center for Humane Technology); Shane Parrish (*Clear Thinking*); James Clear (*Atomic Habits*); Cal Newport (*Deep Work*); Mihaly Csikszentmihalyi (*Flow*); Carol Dweck (*Mindset*); Angela Duckworth (*Grit*); Adam Grant (*Give and Take*); Matthew Walker (*Why We Sleep*); Roy Baumeister (decision fatigue research); Anders Ericsson (deliberate practice research); Peter Gollwitzer (implementation intentions research); BJ

Fogg (*Tiny Habits*); Ethan Kross (*Chatter*); Mark Granovetter (weak ties research); Barry Schwartz (*The Paradox of Choice*); Gerd Gigerenzer (*Risk Savvy*); Scott Adams (*How to Fail at Almost Everything and Still Win Big*); Nathaniel Kleitman (ultradian rhythm research); John Doerr (*Measure What Matters*); Gary Klein, Daniel Kahneman, and the broader research traditions of Cognitive Behavioral Therapy and behavioral finance.

All quotations have been kept brief, attributed, and used solely for purposes of commentary, criticism, and education. Where any reader believes a citation to be incomplete or in error, the publisher welcomes correction at the email address above and will make appropriate updates in subsequent printings.

Trademarks

humbolton.com

Dedication

For Izzy.

Who taught me that building something real

starts with showing up every day,

even when the instructions are wrong

and the parts don't fit.

Especially then.

ABSTRACT

Think and Grow Rich sold over 100 million copies and earned its place in the canon of motivational literature. It also embedded a generation of wealth-builders in metaphysical explanations that were already disputed in 1937 and have not survived contact with modern neuroscience, cognitive psychology, or behavioral economics.

This book preserves Napoleon Hill's structural insight, that durable wealth begins in the mind and is built through deliberate, repeated practice, and replaces every supporting explanation with current, evidence-based mechanisms. Where Hill invoked Infinite Intelligence and cosmic vibrations, the contemporary explanation is neuroplasticity, predictive coding, and the documented behavior of the reticular activating system. Where Hill described the Master Mind as an almost mystical fusion of intelligences, the modern equivalent is a deliberately constructed, mutually accountable peer system that no AI tool can replicate.

The Think Again Loop is the operating framework: a four-phase iterative cycle of **Examine, Design, Execute, and Recalibrate**, running on a 90-day cadence. Each of Hill's original thirteen principles is rebuilt within this structure and grounded in research from Kahneman, Bandura, Munger, Doidge, Lembke, Klein, Duke, Housel, and others. Three additional chapters address what Hill could not have anticipated: the modern wealth stack of income, equity, and leverage in 2026; the neuroplastic and algorithmic war for cognitive sovereignty; and a structured method for evaluating financial advice in a market increasingly populated by AI-generated content with no human accountability behind it.

This book is intended for readers who want the durable insights of the classical self-improvement tradition stripped of its supernatural scaffolding and rebuilt on what is now actually known about how minds, markets, and money interact in the era of artificial intelligence.

Table of Contents

HOW TO USE THIS BOOK

Three minutes. That's all I need. The architecture matters, and understanding it will make everything land harder.

* * *

Every principle maps to one of four phases. Together they form The Think Again Loop:

EXAMINE → DESIGN → EXECUTE → RECALIBRATE

↑↓←←←←←←←←←← ←←←←↑↓

Phase One: Examine. Audit what's already running: default desires, inherited money stories, uncalibrated confidence. Chapters 1 through 3.

Phase Two: Design. Replace the defaults. Build the skill stack, planning system, and revenue architecture. Chapters 4 through 6.

Phase Three: Execute. Decide faster, persist smarter, and confront what the money is actually for. Chapters 7 through 9.

Phase Four: Recalibrate. Build relationships, manage energy, debug cognitive biases, protect your brain, and calibrate intuition. Then loop back with sharper eyes. Chapters 10 through 13.

Chapters 14 and 15 are the foundation and capstone. Chapter 15 is the BS detection system. The loop runs every 90 days. It doesn't end. That's the point.

* * *

Three ways to read this book:

Sequential: Start at the Introduction. The chapters build. This gives you the full architecture.

Triage: Know your problem? Go to that chapter. Can't decide? Chapter 7. Brain fried? Chapters 11 and 12. No idea what you want? Chapter 1.

Exercise-First: Skip to the Appendix. Pick the exercise that matches your most urgent need. Do it. Then read the chapter.

* * *

The exercises are the book. Reading without doing them is watching a cooking show and calling it dinner.

Somewhere around Chapter 5, you'll want to put this book down and go do something. When that happens, go do the thing. The book will wait. The momentum won't.

THE THINK AGAIN LOOP

A One-Page Model

EXAMINE → DESIGN → EXECUTE → RECALIBRATE → (repeat)

	EXAMINE	DESIGN	EXECUTE	RE-CALIBRATE
Purpose	See what's running without your permission	Replace defaults with intentional systems	Act, measure, and learn from feedback	Update the system based on evidence
Key Question	What invisible default is costing me money?	What system replaces it?	What behavior produces evidence?	What does the feedback require me to change?
Failure Mode	Skipping straight to action without auditing	Designing a perfect plan you never execute	Executing without measuring results	Ignoring feedback that contradicts your ego
Key Output	Honest financial baseline and identified blind spots	90-Day Sprint with OKRs and Kill Criteria	Data: what worked, what didn't, what surprised you	Updated plan for the next 90-day cycle
Chapters	1, 2, 3	4, 5, 6	7, 8, 9	10, 11, 12, 13

Key Question What invisible default is costing me money? What system replaces it? What behavior produces evidence? What does the feedback require me to change?

Failure Mode Skipping straight to action without auditing Designing a perfect plan you never execute Executing without measuring results Ignoring feedback that contradicts your ego

Key Output Honest financial baseline and identified blind spots 90-Day Sprint with OKRs and Kill Criteria Data: what worked, what didn't, what surprised you Updated plan for the next 90-day cycle

Purpose See what's running without your permission Replace defaults with intentional systems Act, measure, and learn from feedback Update the system based on evidence

Key Question What invisible default is costing me money? What system replaces it? What behavior produces evidence? What does the feedback require me to change?

Failure Mode Skipping straight to action without auditing Designing a perfect plan you never execute Executing without measuring results Ignoring feedback that contradicts your ego

Key Output Honest financial baseline and identified blind spots 90-Day Sprint with OKRs and Kill Criteria Data: what worked, what didn't, what surprised you Updated plan for the next 90-day cycle

Chapters 1, 2, 3, 4, 5, 6, 7, 8, 9, 10, 11, 12, 13...

The loop runs on a 90-day cadence. At the end of each cycle, you return to Examine with sharper eyes, better data, and a recalibrated thermostat. Wealth isn't built in a single pass. It's built in iterations, and each iteration makes the next one faster.

Chapters 14 (The Modern Wealth Stack) sits outside the loop as the mechanical foundation and the synthesis. Chapter 15 (The Anti-Guru) is the BS detection filter you apply to everything, including this book.

Photocopy these pages. Tape it to your wall.

Come back to it every 90 days.

PART ONE

The Think Again Loop: Examine Your Defaults

INTRODUCTION

Why Your Grandpa's Wealth Book Needs an Update

Napoleon Hill's Think and Grow Rich has sold over 100 million copies. It has been translated into every major language, quoted in approximately four thousand motivational speeches per day, and placed on the nightstand of every ambitious person who has ever owned a nightstand. If you combined all the highlight marks people have made in that book, the yellow ink alone could fill a swimming pool.

I'm not here to tell you it's garbage. It isn't. Hill interviewed hundreds of successful people, distilled their habits into 13 principles, and packaged a philosophy of achievement that has genuinely changed lives for nearly a century.

But I am here to tell you that a book written during the Great Depression by a man with a complicated relationship to factual accuracy might not be your best guide to building wealth in an economy shaped by artificial intelligence, $1.7 trillion in student debt, $400,000 median home prices, and an attention economy designed by behavioral psychologists to keep you scrolling until your dopamine system looks like a tire fire.

The principles are largely right. The explanations are largely wrong. And the gap between "right principle, wrong explanation" is where people get hurt, because they try to execute solid ideas using broken instructions and then blame themselves when it doesn't work.

Hill said your thoughts have power. He attributed that power to cosmic vibrations and something called Infinite Intelligence. Neuroscience says your thoughts literally rewire your neural pathways through neuroplasticity. Same conclusion. One explanation belongs in a peer-reviewed journal. The other belongs in a very enthusiastic Reddit thread.

Hill said you need a burning desire. Behavioral psychology says you need intrinsic motivation paired with what researchers call implementation intentions: specific if-then commitments that link situations to actions. Same starting energy. One framework produces vision boards. The other produces results.

This book takes each of Hill's 13 principles, keeps what works, upgrades what's outdated, and replaces what was always nonsense with something you can actually use. Every chapter gives you the original principle, the modern rebuild backed by research, and a practical exercise you can do this week. Not next year. Not when the stars align. This week.

* * *

A word about who I am, because it matters.

I'm not a billionaire. I don't have a private jet. I've never been invited to Davos, and I suspect if I showed up they'd ask me to park cars. What I have is three master's degrees, decades of experience in corporate education and instructional design, and a front-row seat to how people actually learn, change, and build new behaviors. I've spent my professional life studying the gap between what people know and what they do, and that gap is the most expensive piece of real estate in the human experience.

I've also built things and failed at them. I've made financial decisions that were smart and financial decisions so catastrophically stupid that they should be preserved in a museum as warnings to future generations. I've hired badly, planned poorly, overestimated my abilities, underestimated the market, and learned the sunk cost fallacy by living inside one for two years.

I'm not writing this from the summit. I'm writing it from the trail. And the trail is where the useful information lives, because the people at the summit tend to forget what the climb actually felt like.

* * *

One thing I will not do in this book is pretend that wealth-building is a pure meritocracy. It isn't. Systemic barriers are real. Generational wealth gaps are real. The person who grew up with money has structural advantages that no mindset trick can replicate for someone who didn't. I refuse to insult your intelligence by pretending otherwise.

But I also refuse to tell you that because the system is imperfect, you have no agency. That's not true either, and it's a convenient excuse masquerading as social awareness. The truth lives in the uncomfortable middle: the system is unfair and you still have moves to make. This book lives in that space.

Hill said, "Whatever the mind can conceive and believe, it can achieve."

I'd revise that: Whatever the mind can conceive, validate with evidence, plan systematically, execute with discipline, measure honestly, and iterate based on feedback has a statistically significant probability of working out.

Less poetic. Significantly more useful.

Let's go.

CHAPTER 1

Desire: You Need More Than a Dream Board

Hill's Principle: "Desire is the starting point of all achievement."

I once wanted to be a day trader.

This was around 2014, and I had just read enough about options strategies to be devastatingly dangerous. I had the desire. I had notebooks full of strategies. I had a burning, gut-level, wake-up-excited, Hill-approved yearning to master the markets and achieve financial independence through sheer intellectual force. I was going to crack the code. I was going to out-think Wall Street. I was a man with three master's degrees and a brokerage account, and that combination had never gone wrong in the history of finance. (It has gone wrong constantly in the history of finance.)

I lost money. Not life-ruining money, but enough to fund a decent vacation and a significant amount of humiliation. And the thing that stung wasn't the loss itself. It was the realization that my desire had been enormous, specific, emotionally charged, and almost entirely useless, because desire without a system is just an expensive way to learn you should have had a system.

Napoleon Hill opens Think and Grow Rich by declaring that desire is the starting point of all achievement. He's not wrong. Without wanting something, nothing moves. You don't build a business, develop a skill, or crawl out of bed at an unreasonable hour to work on something difficult unless something inside you is pulling you forward.

But "starting point" is the key phrase, and in the decades since Hill wrote those words, the self-help industry has treated desire as the starting point, the middle, and the finish line. They've sold millions of people on the idea that wanting something hard enough, with sufficient emotional intensity, will cause reality to rearrange itself in your favor. Vision boards. Manifestation journals. Intention-setting ceremonies.

Wanting is not a strategy. Wanting is a neurological state. And neurological states, left to their own devices, are just electricity with opinions.

* * *

A psychologist named Gabriele Oettingen at NYU ran a series of experiments in the early 2000s that should have permanently damaged the vision board industry. She found that positive fantasizing about a desired outcome actually decreases your likelihood of achieving it.

Let that land for a second. The thing everyone tells you to do, the visualization, the vivid mental rehearsal of success, makes you less likely to succeed.

The mechanism is elegant and brutal. When you vividly imagine achieving your goal, your brain can't fully distinguish between imagining and experiencing. It releases some of the same reward neurochemistry, the same satisfying sense of accomplishment, as if you'd actually done the thing. Your brain goes, "Great, mission accomplished. Time to relax." And you do. You relax into the warm bath of imagined success while your actual circumstances remain perfectly unchanged.

Oettingen didn't stop at the diagnosis. She developed a method called WOOP: Wish, Outcome, Obstacle, Plan. You start with the desire. You imagine the best possible outcome. Then, and this is where it diverges from every manifestation course ever sold, you identify the most likely internal obstacle that will derail you. Finally, you create an if-then plan for overcoming that obstacle.

It isn't pretty. There's no cosmic frequency involved. There's just a researcher telling you that your brain is a beautiful liar and you need to plan for the obstacles, not just fantasize about the victories.

* * *

Here's the second problem with raw desire, and it's the one that cost me money in my trading misadventure: most people never translate desire from a feeling into an operation.

Fantasy desire: "I want to be financially free."

Operational desire: "I want to generate $7,500 per month in net income from my freelance consulting practice within 14 months by acquiring eight recurring clients at an average retainer of $950, which requires a close rate of 15% on approximately 54 qualified prospects."

Feel the difference? The first statement is a bumper sticker. The second is a business plan compressed into one sentence. Hill actually understood this distinction. He was specific about writing down the exact amount, the exact deadline, and the exact plan. But that nuance got lost in the cultural game of telephone. By the time his ideas filtered through decades of motivational speakers and Instagram infographics, the message had been reduced to "believe and receive."

Your brain is a search engine, but it needs a specific query. Typing "I want good things" into Google returns 4.2 billion useless results. Typing "B2B consulting client acquisition strategies for mid-market SaaS companies" returns a business. Specificity is the bridge between feeling and building, and the self-help industry burned that bridge so they could sell you candles to hold while you stare at the river.

* * *

Let me bring in a financial dimension here, because this is a wealth book and the desire conversation needs to connect to actual money behavior.

One of the most common things I see in my corporate training work is people who have a vague desire to "be better with money" but have never once sat down and calculated their actual numbers. They don't know their net worth. They don't know their savings rate. They don't know their monthly burn rate to the dollar. They have a relationship with money that is almost entirely emotional and almost zero percent operational.

This is the financial equivalent of wanting to lose weight without ever stepping on a scale. You can't fix what you can't measure, and you can't pursue what you haven't defined. The very first act of directed desire, before vision boards, before manifestation, before any of the sexy stuff, is sitting down with a spreadsheet and looking at reality with both eyes open.

I know that's not inspiring. It's not supposed to be inspiring. It's supposed to be useful. And useful beats inspiring every single time over a long enough horizon.

When I finally got serious about my own financial life, the thing that changed wasn't my desire. I'd always wanted financial independence. The thing that changed was my willingness to look at the actual numbers, acknowledge the gap between where I was and where I wanted to be, and convert that gap into a set of specific, time-bound, measurable behaviors. It was boring. It was uncomfortable. And it was the first financial decision I'd made in years that actually worked.

* * *

Let's talk about dopamine, because the modern world has weaponized this neurotransmitter against your ability to want hard things.

Dopamine isn't the "pleasure chemical." That's a pop-science myth that has been corrected so many times it should be embarrassed to show its face in public. Dopamine is the anticipation chemical. It's the molecule of wanting, not having. Your brain releases it in response to the prediction of a reward, not the reward itself. This is why scrolling social media is addictive: every swipe might reveal something interesting. The might is the dopamine. The slot-machine of maybe.

Andrew Huberman at Stanford has laid this out clearly: dopamine is the currency of motivation. When it flows toward productive goals, you're driven and focused. When it's being hijacked by apps engineered to exploit variable reward schedules, your motivational system gets rerouted. Your brain learns to want easy things. Quick rewards. Low effort. High stimulation.

Building wealth is none of those things. Building wealth is slow, boring, often frustrating, and the rewards are delayed by months or years. If your dopamine system has been trained on the all-you-can-eat buffet of digital stimulation, the delayed gratification required by wealth-building feels like starvation. Not because you lack desire. Because your reward circuitry has been recalibrated to need more stimulation for less effort.

Before you can harness desire in any useful way, you might need to do something Hill never talked about: audit your dopamine diet and start cutting the cheap sources so your brain can actually get excited about the hard, meaningful work that produces real results.

I notice this in my own life. On weeks when I'm disciplined about screen time, when I'm limiting the social media and the news consumption and the mindless scrolling, my ability to sit with difficult work increases dramatically. My tolerance for boredom goes up. My creative output improves. It's not willpower. It's neurochemistry. I've simply stopped flooding my reward system with noise so it can respond to signal.

* * *

The third piece of this puzzle comes from Peter Gollwitzer, who has studied what he calls implementation intentions for decades. The concept is almost offensively simple: it's an if-then statement linking a specific situation to a specific action.

"If it is 6 AM on a weekday, then I spend 45 minutes on my highest-leverage financial task before checking email."

"If a prospect says no, then I ask what it would take to change that answer."

"If I feel the urge to impulse-buy something online, then I add it to a 30-day list and walk away."

Gollwitzer's data shows that people who form these intentions are two to three times more likely to follow through than people who simply set the goal. Two to three times. That's not a marginal edge. That's the difference between a New Year's resolution and an actual behavior change.

Why does it work? Because it removes negotiation from the moment of action. You've already decided. When the situation arises, you don't debate with yourself. You don't wait to "feel like it." The decision was made in advance by your rational self, and your in-the-moment self just executes. It's pre-programming. It's automating yourself.

Here's the financial application: most money mistakes happen in moments of decision fatigue, emotional reactivity, or social pressure. The impulse buy. The unnecessary upgrade. The investment panic-sell. If you've pre-committed your response to those situations, the mistake never gets the chance to happen. You've built a firewall between the trigger and the regret.

I have implementation intentions for my own financial life that have saved me genuinely embarrassing amounts of money. "If I'm considering a purchase over $100, then I wait 72 hours." That single rule has probably saved me $15,000 over the last five years, because it turns out that 72 hours is enough time for approximately 80% of my "I need this" feelings to reveal themselves as "I wanted this for 20 minutes and then forgot it existed."

* * *

So let's rebuild Hill's first principle for a world he wouldn't recognize.

Desire is still the starting point. Without it, nothing moves. But desire by itself is just electricity without a circuit.

Modernized Principle 1: Directed Desire.

First: define the desire in operational terms. Not "I want wealth." The exact amount, the exact timeline, the exact vehicle. Write it down. If you can't write it as one specific sentence with numbers in it, you haven't finished defining it.

Second: run it through WOOP. Imagine the best outcome. Then identify the internal obstacles. Not the external ones you can't control. The internal ones you can. Be honest about what's most likely to stop you. Is it discipline? Fear? Comfort? The gravitational pull of your current lifestyle?

Third: create implementation intentions for each obstacle. If X happens, then I do Y. Pre-commit. Remove the negotiation from the moment.

Fourth: audit your dopamine diet. List your top three sources of cheap stimulation and build a specific plan to reduce each. Not eliminate. Reduce. You're recalibrating, not becoming a monk.

Fifth: look at your actual numbers. Net worth. Monthly income. Monthly expenses. Savings rate.

Debt balances. Look at them. All of them. The desire to build wealth starts with the willingness to see where you actually are.

Sixth: revisit every 90 days. Desire is not static. It evolves as you evolve. Your plan should evolve with it.

* * *

The Spreadsheet Moment

One question worth asking before you write anything down: is this desire actually yours?

In Hill's era, wanting things was relatively personal. Your desires were shaped by your family, your community, your immediate circumstances. The inputs were limited. In 2026, a recommendation algorithm with more behavioral data about you than your closest friends is actively constructing what you want, serving you aspirational content calibrated to your past engagement, your income signals, your demographic profile, and whatever kept you on the platform longest last Tuesday. The algorithm does not love you. It loves your watch time.

The test is simple. Take the financial goal you're about to define and sit with it for 48 hours without opening Instagram, YouTube, or any platform that profits from your desire. Does the goal survive? Does it feel as urgent and specific when it isn't being fed by a feed? If it does, it's yours. If it fades or reshapes significantly, some of what you were pursuing belonged to the algorithm. That distinction is worth the 48 hours of mild withdrawal.

On the practical side: AI tools are now legitimate WOOP partners. Describe your financial goal to a capable model, then prompt it to surface the most likely internal obstacles and stress-test your implementation intentions. An AI has no ego investment in your plan succeeding. It will argue with your assumptions without needing to be polite about it. Your friends, bless them, are still calculating how much honesty they can deliver before brunch gets weird. The model is not.

Let me tell you about the night the spreadsheet changed everything, because it illustrates exactly what directed desire looks like in practice.

It was a Thursday in 2018. Izzy was already asleep. I was at the kitchen table with a laptop, and for the first time in my adult life, I was building a complete financial picture: every account, every debt, every recurring expense, every subscription I'd forgotten about, every automatic payment I'd stopped noticing. It took about three hours.

The number at the bottom of the net worth column was not catastrophic. It was mediocre. And mediocre, when you've been telling yourself you're "doing fine," hits harder than catastrophic, because catastrophic at least has the drama of a crisis. Mediocre is just the quiet accumulation of years of not paying attention.

I found $340 per month in subscriptions I barely used. I found a $2,100 annual insurance premium I'd never compared against alternatives. I found that my actual savings rate, not the one I vaguely believed in but the one the math confirmed, was 4.2%. At that rate, I would reach financial independence approximately never.

That Thursday night spreadsheet became the foundation of everything that followed. Not because it was motivating. It wasn't. It was deflating. But deflation based on reality is infinitely more useful than inflation based on fantasy. The number gave my desire a starting position. Without a starting position, desire is just a feeling with no GPS coordinates.

Within six months of that spreadsheet night, I had eliminated $340/month in waste, renegotiated the insurance premium down by $600/year, automated a 20% savings transfer, and built the implementation intention system I described earlier. None of that required more desire. It required looking at a number I'd been avoiding and letting the number do the motivating.

Your spreadsheet moment is waiting. It might be ugly. It will be useful. And useful, over a long enough timeline, beats inspiring every single time.

* * *

The Desire Audit: This Week's Challenge

I'm not going to call this a worksheet. Worksheets are what HR departments hand out at mandatory training sessions. This is a dare. I dare you to answer these five questions with the kind of honesty that makes you slightly uncomfortable.

One: What exactly do I want to achieve financially in the next 12 months? Write a number. Not "more money." A number. If you can't pick one, you've just learned something important about why nothing has changed yet.

Two: Why do I want this? Not the surface answer. The real one. Keep asking "why" until you hit something that makes your chest tighten. That's the real desire. It's usually about freedom, security, proving something to yourself, or not wanting to repeat a pattern you watched your parents live.

Three: What is the primary internal obstacle that has stopped me before? Not "the economy." Not "my boss." What inside you has been the bottleneck? Name it. Out loud if you're feeling bold.

Four: Write three implementation intentions. If-then format. Link specific situations to specific actions. Make them about money. Make them specific enough that a stranger could follow them.

Five: Check your actual numbers. Right now. Open the banking app, the investment account, the credit card statement. Write down your net worth, your monthly savings rate, and your total debt. If this makes you nauseous, that's the feeling of reality arriving, and it's the most productive nausea you'll ever experience.

Hill gave you permission to want. I'm giving you the blueprint to make wanting useful. And a dare to look at the scoreboard before you start playing the game.

Let's keep going.

CHAPTER 2

Faith: Believing in Yourself Without Being Delusional

Hill's Principle: "Faith is the visualization of, and belief in, the attainment of desire."

Seventy percent of people will experience impostor syndrome at some point in their lives. Seventy percent. That means in any room of ten ambitious, capable, educated professionals, seven of them are quietly convinced that they're frauds and it's only a matter of time before everyone figures it out.

At the same time, research consistently shows that the people who are least competent in a given domain are the most confident about their abilities. The less you know, the less you realize you don't know. Psychologists David Dunning and Justin Kruger documented this in 1999, and the effect named after them has since become one of the most replicated findings in cognitive psychology.

So let me frame the absurdity of our situation: the people who most need confidence don't have it, and the people who have the most confidence are the ones who should have the least. And somewhere in between those two failure modes, Hill is standing with his arms outstretched, shouting, "Just have faith!"

He's not entirely wrong. But "just have faith" without a calibration mechanism is how you end up as either the brilliant professional who won't negotiate for a raise or the guy who pitched a luxury music festival on a private island, charged people $12,000 a ticket, and delivered cheese sandwiches in styrofoam containers.

Billy McFarland, the architect of the Fyre Festival disaster, had faith. He believed so completely in his own vision that he convinced investors, media companies, models, musicians, and ticket-buyers to pour millions of dollars into something that existed almost entirely in his imagination. His faith was burning, unshakable, and Hill-approved. It was also completely disconnected from his competence, his resources, and reality.

The distance between faith and delusion is measured in feedback. And Hill never gave you a ruler.

* * *

Albert Bandura, a psychologist at Stanford, gave us a better framework in 1977 when he coined the term self-efficacy. Self-efficacy is not "believing in yourself" in the vague, poster-on-a-wall sense. It's believing in your ability to execute specific behaviors in specific situations to produce specific outcomes.

Notice the precision. Not "I'm great." Not "I can do anything." Instead: "I can write a compelling proposal for this specific client because I've done similar work four times, I understand their industry, and I've rehearsed the pitch with someone who gave me honest feedback."

Bandura identified four sources of self-efficacy, and they're essentially a recipe for building real confidence instead of performing fake confidence.

Mastery experiences. You've done the thing before and it worked. This is the strongest source by far.

Nothing builds belief like a receipt. When I look back at the moments in my career where my confidence was highest, it was never after reading a motivational book or attending a seminar. It was after delivering a project that worked. After getting a result I could point to. After having evidence, not affirmation.

Vicarious experience. You've watched someone whose starting position was similar to yours pull it off. Not a billionaire. Not someone born into advantages you don't have. Someone who started roughly where you are and built something real. This is why representation matters in business, in media, in leadership. If you've never seen someone who looks like you, sounds like you, or came from where you came from succeed at the thing you're attempting, your brain has a harder time computing the possibility.

Verbal persuasion. Someone credible told you that you can do this. The key word is credible. Your mom telling you you're brilliant is lovely. Your mentor who has built three businesses telling you your plan is sound is useful. The source determines the weight.

Physiological state. When you're rested, healthy, and emotionally regulated, belief comes easier. When you're running on four hours of sleep, a liter of coffee, and ambient dread, everything feels impossible. Your beliefs are downstream of your biology, which is why the energy management chapter later in this book isn't a luxury. It's infrastructure.

The beauty of Bandura's framework is that it converts "have more faith" into a checklist. Have I done this before? Have I seen someone like me do it? Do I have credible people in my corner? Am I in a physical state that supports belief? If most of those answers are no, you don't have a faith problem. You have a preparation problem. And preparation is fixable.

* * *

Let me tell you about a time my confidence was badly miscalibrated, because I think it illustrates both sides of this problem.

Early in my career, I was asked to facilitate a training session for a group of senior executives. I had the knowledge. I'd designed the content. But I was 15 years younger than the youngest person in the room, and every cell in my body was screaming that I didn't belong there. Classic impostor syndrome. High competence, low confidence.

I almost declined the opportunity. I had a dozen reasons prepared: scheduling conflicts, not the right fit, someone else would be better. All lies. The real reason was fear. The real reason was a voice in my head that said, "They'll see through you."

I did the session anyway, mostly because my boss didn't give me a choice. And it went well. Not perfectly. But well enough that two of the executives requested me specifically for their next training cycle. That mastery experience, that piece of evidence, did more for my confidence than every motivational poster I'd ever read combined.

Now contrast that with a business investment I made a few years later, where my confidence was too high. I'd had a few wins. I was feeling smart. I put money into a venture that a more experienced investor would have flagged as risky, because I'd graduated from impostor syndrome directly into Dunning-Kruger territory. I knew enough to feel confident but not enough to know what I was missing. The investment underperformed badly, and the tuition was expensive.

Both failures, the under-confidence and the over-confidence, had the same root cause: I wasn't calibrating. I was just feeling. And feelings, unexamined, are a terrible basis for financial decisions.

* * *

Carol Dweck's mindset research deserves a mention here, and also a warning.

Dweck showed that people who believe their abilities can be developed through effort and strategy (a growth mindset) outperform people who believe their abilities are fixed and innate. This is robust, well-replicated research, and it's genuinely useful for anyone who has internalized the belief that they're "not a money person" or "not smart enough" to build wealth.

You are not locked into your current financial identity. Your ability to understand investing, negotiate salary, manage cash flow, build a business? All developable. All teachable. The neural pathways that currently say "I can't" are just pathways, and pathways can be rebuilt with evidence and practice.

Here's the warning: the pop-culture version of growth mindset has been distorted into "you can do anything if you believe and try hard enough," which is not what Dweck said. Growth mindset means your limits are further out than you think and can be expanded through strategy and feedback. It does not mean limits don't exist. It does not mean effort alone is sufficient. It means effort plus strategy plus feedback plus honest self-assessment can move you further than you expected. That's a meaningful claim. It's also a far cry from "just believe."

* * *

The financial application of calibrated confidence is worth spelling out, because this is where abstract psychology converts into actual money.

Salary negotiation. Research consistently shows that people who negotiate their starting salary earn significantly more over their lifetime than those who accept the first offer. The gap compounds over decades. And the number one reason people don't negotiate? They don't believe they're worth more. Not because they aren't. Because their confidence hasn't been calibrated against market data. They're running on feeling instead of evidence.

Before any salary negotiation, build your evidence file. What are comparable roles paying? (Use data, not guesses.) What specific results have you delivered? What's the quantified impact of your work? When you walk into that conversation armed with evidence, your confidence isn't faith. It's a spreadsheet with a spine.

Investment decisions. Overconfidence in investing is one of the most expensive cognitive errors documented. Barber and Odean's research on individual investors showed that the most active traders (the most confident ones, who believed they could beat the market through superior analysis) underperformed passive investors by significant margins. They traded more, incurred more fees and taxes, and made more emotionally driven decisions. Their faith in their own judgment was sincere, well-articulated, and financially destructive.

The antidote: know your circle of competence. If you genuinely understand an investment, proceed with proportional confidence. If you're investing based on a feeling, a tip, or a YouTube video you watched at 1 AM, your confidence is Dunning-Kruger in a brokerage account.

* * *

There is a newer and particularly seductive variant of this effect worth naming: AI-assisted Dunning-Kruger.

When you can present AI-generated output as your own thinking, whether it lands in a pitch deck, a financial analysis, or a business strategy, you can perform competence at a level that bears no relationship to your actual ability to execute when the tool isn't in the room. The gap between performed expertise and earned expertise has never been easier to widen. It has also never been more expensive when it collapses under real pressure, which it will, usually in the meeting that matters most.

The antidote is unchanged: mastery experiences, honest feedback, and the kind of competence that survives when the tool is unavailable. Self-efficacy built on AI-generated performance is a Jenga tower in a wind tunnel. It looks impressive right up until the moment it doesn't.

* * *

Cognitive Behavioral Therapy provides the most practical tool for recalibrating beliefs that I've encountered anywhere in psychology.

The core insight of CBT is devastatingly simple: your thoughts are not facts. The stories you tell yourself about who you are, what you deserve, and what you're capable of are narratives, not truths. And narratives can be edited.

The process: when you catch a belief that's undermining you ("I'm not the kind of person who builds wealth," "I'll never understand investing," "people like me don't get ahead"), run it through three questions. What is the evidence for this thought? What is the evidence against it? What would I say to a friend who told me this about themselves?

That third question is the killer. You would never tell a friend that they're destined to be broke. You would never tell a friend that they're too dumb to learn investing. You would never tell a friend to stop trying. So why are you saying these things to yourself with the authority of settled fact?

CBT doesn't make negative thoughts disappear. It loosens their grip. It turns an absolute ("I can't") into a hypothesis ("I haven't yet, and here's what I could try"). And hypotheses, unlike absolutes, can be tested.

* * *

Sincero's Big Snooze and Eker's Financial Thermostat

Jen Sincero, in You Are a Badass at Making Money, describes something she calls the Big Snooze: the part of your identity that actively resists change. When you start growing, earning more, thinking bigger, a voice inside pushes back. It says you're getting too big for your britches. It reminds you of every failure. It manufactures anxiety about success dressed up as humility.

The clinical explanation: your brain is a prediction machine that values stability over improvement. Status quo bias isn't just a financial decision-making error. It's an identity-maintenance system. Your current financial self-concept is a neural pathway that resists disruption the same way any entrenched habit does.

I've felt the Big Snooze every time I've tried to level up financially. When my income crossed a certain threshold, I noticed an almost physical discomfort, a sense that I was breaking some unspoken rule about what people like me were supposed to earn. I started self-sabotaging: overcommitting to free work, underpricing services, making impulsive purchases that conveniently kept my savings right around the level I was unconsciously comfortable with.

I negotiated a 22% increase at a job transition by walking in with three pages of market data and quantified project results. My gut said to take whatever they offered. My evidence file said I was undervaluing myself by $18,000. The evidence file won. The Big Snooze screamed the entire time. I ignored it.

* * *

The Confidence Calibration: This Week's Challenge

This takes 20 minutes. It might be the most honest 20 minutes you spend this month. Fair warning: honesty doesn't always feel good. It does, however, always feel useful eventually.

Pick the financial or professional goal that matters most to you right now. The one that's either keeping you up at night or the one you've been avoiding thinking about because thinking about it makes you feel like a fraud.

Rate your competence for that goal on a scale of 1 to 10. Use evidence. List the specific skills, experiences, and knowledge you actually have. Not what you wish you had. What you have.

Rate your confidence for that goal on the same scale. How much do you believe, gut-level, that you'll actually pull this off?

Compare the numbers. If competence is significantly higher than confidence, welcome to impostor syndrome. Your homework: build an evidence file. Every relevant accomplishment. Every piece of positive feedback from a credible source. Every time you've done something hard and it worked. Read it when the voice in your head starts lying to you.

If confidence is significantly higher than competence, welcome to Dunning-Kruger. Your homework: find someone who has done what you're trying to do and ask them, "What am I not seeing?" Then actually listen to the answer instead of waiting for your turn to explain why your plan is brilliant.

If the numbers are close, you're in the sweet spot. Your homework: stay there by maintaining feedback loops. The moment you stop getting honest input is the moment the numbers start drifting.

Identify one thought that undermines your financial confidence. Write it down. Run it through the CBT filter. Write the revised, evidence-based version. Put it somewhere you'll see it daily. Not as an affirmation. As a correction.

Faith isn't summoned from the ether. It's engineered from evidence, calibrated with feedback, and maintained through honest self-assessment. Hill had the right instinct. We've just got better tools now.

CHAPTER 3

Autosuggestion: Reprogramming Your Brain

(Without the Cult Stuff)

Hill's Principle: "Autosuggestion is the medium for influencing the subconscious mind."

What is the first thing you thought about money this morning?

Not the first financial decision you made. The first thought. The first narrative that drifted through your mind before the coffee kicked in and the day's noise took over. Did it sound like "I need to check my account" (anxiety)? "Another day, another dollar" (resignation)? "I have a plan and it's working" (agency)?

Most people have never examined their default money narrative because it runs so constantly that it's become invisible, like the hum of a refrigerator. You stop hearing it. But it's still shaping everything: your spending behavior, your willingness to negotiate, your tolerance for financial risk, your ability to delay gratification, your entire emotional relationship with the number in your bank account.

Napoleon Hill's third principle is autosuggestion: the practice of feeding specific thoughts to your subconscious through repeated verbal and emotional emphasis. Read your goals aloud. Feel the emotion of already having what you want. Let the vibration of certainty penetrate your subconscious until it manifests your desires.

And if you are currently standing in your bathroom every morning saying "I am wealthy, I am powerful, I am a money magnet" while your checking account has $214 in it, I need to tell you something with love: you are not programming your subconscious for success. You are lying to yourself in a steamy room while your toothbrush silently judges you.

* * *

Joanne Wood and her colleagues at the University of Waterloo tested this directly in 2009. They had participants repeat the affirmation "I am a lovable person" and measured the effects on self-esteem.

People who already felt good about themselves felt slightly better. People with low self-esteem felt worse. The affirmation backfired.

The mechanism: when you state something you fundamentally don't believe, your brain argues with you. You say "I am wealthy" and your brain fires back with the unpaid bills, the declining savings, the student loans, the memory of every financial mistake you've made since 2017. The dissonance between the statement and the reality doesn't resolve in the statement's favor. It reinforces the reality.

So does this mean you're stuck with the money story you have? Absolutely not. It means you need a better method than contradicting yourself in the mirror.

* * *

Neuroplasticity is the method, and it's the scientific discovery Hill would have built his entire book around if he'd had access to it.

Your brain physically restructures itself based on what you repeatedly do, think, and experience. Norman Doidge documented this exhaustively in The Brain That Changes Itself: stroke patients who relearned abilities by training undamaged brain regions to take over destroyed ones. Elderly patients growing new neural connections by learning instruments and languages. The brain is not hardware. It's clay. Constantly being molded.

The principle that matters: neurons that fire together wire together. When you repeatedly practice a behavior, engage a thought pattern, or inhabit a mental state, the neural pathway for that pattern gets faster, stronger, and more automatic. This is how habits form. How skills develop. And how beliefs become so embedded that they feel like unchangeable features of your identity.

Your belief that you're "bad with money" is not a fact about you. It's a neural pathway that was built by repeated experience, reinforcement from your environment, and years of practice. It can be rebuilt. But the rebuilding requires action, not affirmation.

* * *

Let me give you three evidence-based reprogramming methods that actually work, along with the financial behavior each one targets.

Method one: Self-distanced self-talk.

Ethan Kross at the University of Michigan showed that talking to yourself in the third person or using your own name produces significantly better emotional regulation and performance than first-person self-talk. Saying "Ken can handle this negotiation" works better than "I can handle this negotiation" because it creates psychological distance. Your brain treats third-person self-talk as if it's coming from an external advisor, and you are almost always wiser when advising someone else than when advising yourself.

Financial application: before any high-stakes money conversation (salary negotiation, investor pitch, big purchase decision, confronting a business partner about finances), take 60 seconds and coach yourself by name. "Ken has prepared for this. He knows his numbers. He's going to present the data and let the data do the work." It sounds absurd. The research says it works. I use it. It works.

Method two: Behavioral evidence stacking.

This comes from James Clear's identity-based habit framework. Instead of setting a goal ("save $10,000"), define the identity ("I'm a person who manages money deliberately") and then stack small behaviors that provide evidence for that identity.

Automate a $50 weekly transfer to savings. Evidence. Check your net worth on the first of every month. Evidence. Negotiate a lower rate on one recurring bill. Evidence. Cook dinner instead of ordering delivery three times this week. Evidence. Say no to one purchase you would have mindlessly made. Evidence.

Each action is tiny. Each one is nearly insignificant in isolation. But each sends a signal to your subconscious: "This is who we are now." And over weeks and months, those signals compound. The new pathway strengthens. The old one ("I'm bad with money") weakens from disuse. You didn't affirm your way to a new identity. You behaved your way there.

I started doing this three years ago when I realized that my financial self-concept was lagging behind my actual financial behavior. I was making decent money and making decent decisions, but I still felt like the broke kid who grew up watching his parents stress about bills. The identity hadn't caught up. So I started deliberately noticing every financially competent thing I did. Not celebrating it like I'd won the lottery. Just noticing it. Registering it. Letting my brain count the evidence. Over about six months, the internal narrative shifted from "I'm figuring this out" to "I know what I'm doing." The evidence made the shift possible. The affirmation alone never could have.

Method three: Habit stacking.

BJ Fogg at Stanford developed Tiny Habits around an elegantly simple structure: "After I [existing habit], I will [new tiny behavior]."

After I pour my morning coffee, I review my financial dashboard for 60 seconds. After I sit down at my desk, I write one paragraph of my business plan. After I put my kids to bed, I spend 10 minutes on my side project. After I open my banking app, I move $10 to savings.

The genius is that it hijacks existing neural architecture. Your morning coffee routine is already a strong pathway. By attaching a new financial behavior to it, you're drafting behind an established habit. The cue is automatic. The new behavior is tiny enough to be frictionless. And over time, the tiny behavior grows because the pathway has been built incrementally, without willpower, without motivation, without standing in front of a mirror hoping the universe is listening.

* * *

Hill got one thing right about autosuggestion that the research purists sometimes undervalue: emotion matters.

Emotionally charged experiences are encoded more deeply and more durably in memory. The amygdala flags emotionally significant events for the hippocampus, essentially stamping them with a “remember this” tag. Events without emotional charge are processed as background noise.

This means that when you're doing behavioral evidence stacking, it helps to actually feel something about it. When you automate that savings transfer, take a second to feel the satisfaction. When you negotiate that bill down, let yourself feel the competence. When you say no to the impulse buy, feel the strength in that choice.

You're not manufacturing fake emotion about a fake outcome, which is what mirror affirmations attempt. You're attaching real emotion to real evidence. That's the difference. And it's the difference between a belief system built on wishes and a belief system built on a foundation that can bear weight.

* * *

One more enemy of effective reprogramming that Hill couldn't have anticipated: the algorithm.

In Hill's era, the stories you told yourself about money were shaped by your family, your community, and maybe a few books. The inputs were limited and relatively stable.

Today, your financial narratives are being actively sculpted by recommendation algorithms designed to maximize engagement. If you follow financial content, the algorithm shows you 23-year-olds who "retired" with crypto gains, lifestyle influencers whose "passive income" is mostly sponsored posts, and hustle accounts that make you feel simultaneously inadequate and guilty for sleeping. If you follow news, the algorithm feeds you housing market doom, economic anxiety, and stories designed to make you either panicked or paralyzed.

Either way, the algorithm is doing Hill's autosuggestion for you. It's programming your subconscious every day. It's just not programming it for success. It's programming it for engagement, which means anxiety, comparison, and emotional reactivity.

Any serious attempt to rewrite your internal money narrative must include a serious audit of your external information diet. You cannot build new pathways if the old ones are being reinforced 47 times a day by your phone.

* * *

The Financial Thermostat

T. Harv Eker, in Secrets of the Millionaire Mind, introduced a concept that maps perfectly onto neuroscience: the financial thermostat. Your subconscious has a "set point" for wealth, just like a thermostat has a set point for temperature. If your internal thermostat is set to $50,000, you'll unconsciously sabotage yourself whenever you earn significantly more, and hustle harder whenever you drop below. Lottery winners go broke because their thermostat is set to middle class. People who dig out of debt go back into debt because their thermostat is set to "owing."

Strip away the seminar packaging and what you have is neuroplasticity: your brain has a deeply wired pattern around a specific financial identity, and that pattern resists disruption. When your income or net worth deviates too far from the set point, your brain generates anxiety, impulsive spending, or self-sabotage to bring you back to "normal."

I watched this in my own life with uncomfortable clarity. For years, my savings would grow to a certain level and then something would happen: an impulsive purchase, an unnecessary expense that conveniently cost just enough to bring me back to my familiar financial baseline. These felt like bad luck. They were behavioral patterns. My thermostat was running, and I didn't know it existed.

The good news: thermostats can be recalibrated. That's literally what behavioral evidence stacking does. Each piece of evidence nudges the set point. The thermostat doesn't move because you told it to. It moves because the accumulated evidence becomes so overwhelming that the old set point can no longer hold.

* * *

The Narrative Rewrite: This Week's Challenge

Three parts. Do all three. Don't skip to the one that sounds easiest.

Part one: The Story Audit. Write down the three deepest stories you carry about money. The ones running on autopilot. Common ones: "My family was never good with money." "You have to be lucky." "I'm too old to start." "Money changes people." "I don't deserve it." Get them out of your head and onto paper. They lose about 40 percent of their power the moment they're visible.

Part two: The Evidence Challenge. For each story, find three specific pieces of evidence from your own life that contradict it. Not from a billionaire's biography. From your life. Times you were good with money. Times luck wasn't the factor. Times you started something late and it worked anyway. If you can't find three, that's data too. It means you need to start generating evidence, and method two above tells you how.

Part three: The Replacement. For each old story, write a new one that you can actually believe. Not "I am a millionaire." Your brain will reject that and make you feel worse. Instead: "I am actively building financial competence, and the evidence is growing every week." Anchor the new narrative in present action, not future fantasy. Then reinforce it daily using your own name: "Ken is building something real. He's not where he wants to be yet, but the trend line is moving in the right direction, and he's got the receipts to prove it."

Hill told you to repeat your goals until your subconscious believed them. The upgrade: live your goals in tiny daily actions, rewrite the stories with evidence, and protect your inputs from the engagement machine.

Same principle. Better execution. No mirror required.

CHAPTER 4

Specialized Knowledge: Google Doesn't Count

Hill's Principle: "Knowledge is only potential power."

Here is the most expensive misconception of the information age: knowing about something and being good at something are the same thing.

They are not. They have never been. And the internet, which has given every human on earth access to virtually all accumulated knowledge, has made the confusion worse, not better, because it has created a generation of people who are spectacularly informed and spectacularly stuck.

I know this because I used to be one of them.

Around 2006, I walked into a Borders bookstore (a moment of silence, please), bought a book on real estate investing, read it cover to cover, and decided I was now a real estate investor. I could throw around terms like "cap rate" and "cash-on-cash return" and "1031 exchange" at dinner parties. People would nod respectfully. I had the vocabulary, the frameworks, and the confidence of a man who had read exactly one book about a subject and mistaken that for competence.

I was not a real estate investor. I was a person who had read a book. And the distance between those two things is where a lot of money goes to die.

Napoleon Hill's fourth principle might be his most prescient. He said knowledge is only potential power, that it becomes actual power only when organized into definite plans of action and directed toward a definite end. He drew a hard line between general knowledge (knowing things) and specialized knowledge (knowing how to apply things in a specific domain to produce specific results).

In 1937, that was a sophisticated insight. In 2026, it's a survival skill.

* * *

The Knowledge Trap works like this: you take a course that recommends another course, which leads to a YouTube series, which introduces a new framework, which has a subreddit devoted to debating its merits, which links to three podcasts, and four months later you've consumed 500 hours of content and produced exactly nothing.

The Knowledge Trap feels productive. That's its superpower. Learning feels like work. Taking a course feels like progress. Reading a book (like this one, and yes, I appreciate the irony) feels like investment. And sometimes it is. But only when the learning is being converted into application. Without application, learning is entertainment wearing a graduation cap.

I spent two years in a knowledge trap around online business. I took courses on SEO, email marketing, funnel building, copywriting, social media strategy, and paid advertising. I could have taught a graduate seminar on digital marketing theory. I had launched exactly zero digital marketing campaigns. The courses were my procrastination dressed in professional development clothing.

The escape came when I finally asked myself a question that I now ask about every learning investment: "What specific project am I going to apply this to within the next 30 days?" If the answer is "nothing specific," the course is procrastination. If the answer is a concrete project with a concrete deadline, the course is preparation. The question isn't whether the knowledge is good. The question is whether I'm using learning as a launchpad or a hiding place.

* * *

Anders Ericsson spent his career studying what separates world-class performers from everyone else. His answer wasn't more knowledge. It was deliberate practice, and its four components are allergic to comfort.

It targets specific weaknesses, not strengths. Most people practice what they're already good at because it feels rewarding. Deliberate practice attacks the thing you're worst at because that's where the growth lives. In financial terms: if you're great at earning but terrible at investing, deliberate practice means spending your learning time on investing, not reading another book about productivity.

It involves immediate feedback. You do the thing and find out quickly whether it worked. This means putting your work in front of people who will be honest, not your mom, not your best friend, not a yes-person. Someone who has done what you're trying to do and will tell you where you're falling short.

It operates at your edge. Not so easy it's boring. Not so hard it's demoralizing. Right at the boundary where you fail about 15 to 20 percent of the time.

Researchers call this the Zone of Proximal Development. I call it the place where growth lives and comfort dies.

It's mentally exhausting. Genuine deliberate practice can only be sustained for about four hours per day, even by elite performers. If you're "studying" for ten hours and it doesn't feel exhausting, you're doing something easier and calling it practice.

* * *

Scott Adams introduced a concept that has become one of the most useful frameworks in my own financial life: the skill stack.

Adams argued that you don't need to be world-class at any single thing. You need to be genuinely good at two or three complementary things that, combined, create a value proposition that almost nobody else has.

The math is compelling. Being in the top 1% of any single skill is extraordinarily hard. Tens of thousands of hours. Genetic advantages often required. But being in the top 25% of three complementary skills? Achievable with focused effort. And the intersection of those three skills creates a space that's uniquely yours, where competition is thin because almost nobody else has that exact combination.

Let me make this concrete with real examples I've encountered in my career.

A physical therapist who understood content marketing and could write clearly built a telehealth education platform serving a niche that the big players ignored. She wasn't the best PT, the best marketer, or the best writer. The intersection made her uncopyable.

A corporate trainer (hi) who understood behavioral psychology and could design curriculum built a career that combines instructional design with cognitive science in a way that most instructional designers can't match. Not because I'm a genius. Because I deliberately stacked skills that multiply each other.

An accountant who learned data visualization and public speaking became a financial educator with a six-figure YouTube channel. An accountant. On YouTube. Making it work. Because the skill stack created a persona that didn't exist before he built it.

Your skill stack is your moat. In a world where AI can do any single skill at a competent level, the human who combines skills in novel ways is the one the machines can't replace.

* * *

Cal Newport's concept of deep work deserves space here because it's the delivery mechanism for everything else in this chapter.

Deep work is cognitively demanding, distraction-free concentration on a task that produces real output. It is the opposite of checking email, attending status meetings, and toggling between Slack tabs. And it is systematically being destroyed by the modern work environment.

Research shows it takes an average of 23 minutes to fully re-engage with a task after an interruption. If you're interrupted eight times in a workday, you're losing three hours of productive cognitive capacity. Not three hours of time. Three hours of the kind of focused cognition that produces skill development, creative work, and real output.

The financial implication is direct: your ability to do deep work is itself a specialized skill, and one of the most valuable you can develop. Most of your competition can't do it. They're too busy checking their phones. If you can carve out two to three hours of genuinely undistracted deep work per day, you will outproduce most people who "work" twice as many hours. I've tested this in my own life. On days with two solid deep work blocks, I produce more meaningful output than on days with eight hours of fragmented availability.

The practical application: schedule deep work like a meeting. Put it on the calendar. Close the door. Turn off notifications. Put your phone in another room. Not on silent in your pocket. In another room. The physical distance matters because every vibration your phone makes in your pocket is your brain's attention system going on alert, even when you don't look at it.

* * *

The AI question is unavoidable in a chapter about knowledge, so let me address it directly: if a machine can access and apply more knowledge than any human, what's the point of specialized knowledge?

The answer is that AI changes the type of knowledge that matters without eliminating the need for it. AI is extraordinarily good at executing within defined parameters. It is not good at defining the parameters. It can write a business plan and increasingly approximate the strategic judgment of whether the business should exist, but it cannot replace the judgment that comes from skin in the game, irreplaceable contextual relationships, and the lived experience of having been wrong in this specific market before. It can analyze data; it can't tell you which question to ask. It can produce a hundred marketing headlines; it can't tell you which one your specific audience will trust.

The specialized knowledge of the AI era is judgment. The ability to ask the right question. The ability to evaluate output and know when the machine is wrong. (It is wrong sometimes, and it's wrong with extraordinary confidence, which makes it even more dangerous.) The ability to synthesize information across domains and make decisions under genuine uncertainty, where the data is incomplete and the stakes are real.

This is why the skill stack matters more, not less, in the age of AI. AI can do any single skill at a competent level. It cannot combine skills with the contextual judgment that comes from lived experience in a specific domain. Your unique combination of skills, experiences, relationships, and hard-won pattern recognition is the thing the machine can't replicate. Invest in it accordingly.

* * *

From Knowledge to Income: A Worked Example

Let me walk you through how deliberate practice and skill stacking actually convert to money, because abstract frameworks are useful only when they're concrete.

When I recognized my skill stack (instructional design + behavioral psychology + writing), I didn't immediately know how to monetize the intersection. The stack existed. The market for it didn't obviously exist. Nobody was posting job listings for "behavioral psychology-informed instructional designer who also writes in a conversational voice."

So I ran a 90-day experiment. I wrote three articles applying behavioral science principles to corporate training problems. Topics like: why your compliance training doesn't work (hint: it violates every principle of adult learning theory), how to design onboarding that actually changes behavior, why most e-learning is expensive screensaver content. I published them on LinkedIn.

The articles did modestly well. More importantly, they attracted exactly the right attention: L&D directors at mid-sized companies who were frustrated with their training vendors and recognized themselves in the problems I described. Two of them reached out. One became a consulting client. The other became a referral source that generated three more clients over the following year.

Total investment: approximately 30 hours of writing over 90 days. Total return: over $40,000 in consulting revenue in the first year, from a skill stack I already had but hadn't positioned at its most valuable intersection.

That's the skill stack in action. Not a theoretical exercise. A concrete example of identifying the intersection, testing it with minimal investment, and letting the market tell you whether it works. The knowledge was always there. The application was the missing piece. And application, as Hill said 90 years ago, is where potential power becomes actual power.

* * *

The Skill Stack Audit: This Week's Challenge

This exercise maps your unique value proposition. Grab something to write with. Give it 30 honest minutes.

List every skill you have that's at a 6 out of 10 or higher. Not just professional skills. Everything. Cooking. Writing. Public speaking. Data analysis. Negotiation. Teaching. Design. Sales. Managing people. Foreign languages. Fixing things. Whatever you're genuinely decent at, it goes on the list. Be generous. Most people undercount their skills by about 40 percent because they don't recognize abilities they take for granted.

Circle the three that, combined, create the most interesting and valuable intersection. The test: who else has this exact combination? If the answer is "almost nobody," you've found your stack.

For each skill in your stack, rate your current level honestly (beginner, intermediate, advanced) and identify one specific action, not a course, an action with a deliverable and a deadline, that would advance you one level within 90 days.

Identify the one gap skill that would make your stack dramatically more valuable. Not the trendiest skill. Not the one your LinkedIn feed says is hot. The skill that, layered onto what you already have, creates disproportionate value. That's your learning priority for the next quarter.

Build one deep work block into your daily schedule. Minimum 90 minutes. Dedicated to advancing your stack. Put it on your calendar. Treat it as non-negotiable. If someone asks to schedule over it, tell them you have a meeting with your most important client. You do. It's your future earning potential.

And one final instruction, from someone who has bought enough unused online courses to furnish a very small, very shameful library: if you're about to buy a course, ask yourself what specific project you'll apply it to within 30 days. If you don't have an answer, close the browser. Go build something. The knowledge you actually need will reveal itself through the building. It always does.

PART TWO

The Think Again Loop: Design Your System

CHAPTER 5

Imagination: Creative Problem-Solving in the Age of AI

Hill's Principle: "The imagination is the workshop of the mind."

The best business idea I ever had came from a conversation about mushrooms.

I was having dinner with a friend who runs a small mycology operation, growing specialty mushrooms for restaurants. He was talking about his substrate costs. I was thinking about instructional design, because that's what I do and I am incapable of turning it off. Somewhere between his second beer and my third, my brain made a connection that had no business existing: his distribution problem (getting fragile product to chefs fast) looked structurally identical to a knowledge delivery problem I was solving for a corporate client (getting perishable training content to regional managers before it became outdated).

The specifics aren't important. What's important is that the connection came from colliding two completely unrelated domains. Mushroom logistics and corporate training have nothing obvious in common. But the pattern underneath, time-sensitive distribution of perishable value, was the same. And recognizing that pattern produced an idea that neither conversation alone could have generated.

That's imagination. Not divine inspiration. Not a mystical download from the cosmos. It's the trained ability to see structural similarities between things that nobody else is comparing. And it is, in my experience, the most financially valuable cognitive skill that almost nobody deliberately practices.

* * *

Napoleon Hill called imagination "the workshop of the mind" and split it into two types. Synthetic imagination rearranges existing ideas into new combinations. Creative imagination receives flashes of insight from Infinite Intelligence.

Strip away the metaphysics and you're left with a distinction that creativity researchers have validated repeatedly. Arthur Koestler, in The Act of Creation, called it "bisociation": the act of connecting two previously unrelated frames of reference. Humor works this way. Scientific breakthroughs work this way. And nearly every significant business innovation in the last century works this way.

Uber bisociated GPS technology with the taxi industry. Airbnb bisociated vacation rentals with a social trust platform. Warby Parker bisociated direct-to-consumer distribution with premium eyewear. Peloton bisociated boutique fitness with streaming technology. In each case, nobody invented anything new. They saw a connection that nobody else had seen yet and built a business in the gap.

This kind of creativity can't be outsourced to AI. Not because AI isn't creative (it can generate a staggering volume of competent ideas), but because AI's creativity converges toward the center of what already exists. It's the statistical mean in a creative costume. AI can give you 50 variations on existing themes. It struggles to produce the idea that makes all 50 irrelevant.

Your advantage isn't speed or volume. Your advantage is weirdness. The ability to make connections that don't obviously belong together, informed by lived experience, emotional intelligence, and the kind of cross-domain pattern recognition that comes from actually being a human who has had a life.

* * *

Teresa Amabile at Harvard Business School has studied creativity for over 40 years. Her definition is worth memorizing: creativity is the production of ideas that are both novel and useful. Two criteria. Both required.

AI is increasingly good at useful. Humans remain dramatically better at novel. And the financial premium lives in novelty. Useful but unoriginal gets you a commodity. Useful and novel gets you a market.

So how do you train novelty? Three principles from the research, each with a financial application.

Principle one: Consume widely and weirdly.

Steve Jobs credited his creativity to having a broader range of inputs than most people. He studied calligraphy, which later influenced the typography of the Macintosh. He traveled to India, which shaped his aesthetic minimalism. He obsessed over architecture, music, philosophy, and industrial design. His combinatorial palette was enormous because he deliberately fed it from unusual sources.

If you only consume content from your own industry, your combinatorial possibilities are limited. You're trying to make new recipes from the same six ingredients. The financial professional who also reads neuroscience, watches Korean cinema, listens to podcasts about urban agriculture, and plays strategy board games has a dramatically larger idea space than the financial professional who only reads financial content.

This isn't a nice-to-have. This is creative infrastructure. I make a deliberate practice of reading at least one book per month from a domain completely unrelated to my work. Not because I expect direct applicability. Because I'm feeding the bisociation engine. Every domain I understand, even superficially, is another ingredient available for collision.

Principle two: Create constraints.

This sounds counterintuitive. Shouldn't imagination be unconstrained? The research says no. Decades of creativity studies show that constraints boost creative output. When everything is possible, nothing is urgent. When you have limitations, your brain is forced to find solutions within boundaries, and those solutions are consistently more creative than what emerges from unlimited freedom.

Dr. Seuss wrote Green Eggs and Ham using only 50 different words on a bet. Twitter's 140-character limit spawned an entirely new communication form. The sonnet's 14-line structure didn't limit Shakespeare. It focused him.

Financial application: instead of brainstorming "how could I make more money" (infinite, unfocused, paralyzing), constrain the question. "How could I generate $500 per month using only skills I already have, within 90 days, without quitting my job?" The constraints don't shrink the answer. They sharpen the question.

Principle three: Schedule recovery.

The best ideas rarely arrive during focused work. They arrive in the shower, on a walk, while driving, at 3 AM. This isn't mystical. It's your default mode network, the brain system that activates when you're not focused on a specific task. This network makes associative connections in the background, linking pieces of information you've consumed but haven't consciously connected.

The implication: after concentrated creative or analytical work, deliberately step away. Walk. Exercise. Do something mechanical and unrelated. The stepping away isn't wasted time. It's when your background processor does its best work.

I write my best instructional content on days when I alternate between focused writing blocks and 20-minute walks. Not because walking is magical. Because the walking gives my default mode network time to process what I was writing and surface connections I hadn't consciously made. My best paragraph of the day almost always arrives in my head during a walk, not at the keyboard.

* * *

Creating vs. Competing

Wallace Wattles wrote The Science of Getting Rich in 1910, and buried inside its dated language is an idea that has become more relevant with each passing decade: wealth comes from creation, not competition.

Wattles argued that competing for existing market share is a losing game because competition drives margins to zero and turns business into a war of attrition. Creating new value, seeing opportunities nobody else sees and building something that didn't exist before, is the only sustainable path to wealth.

In the AI era, this distinction has become critical. AI can compete: it optimizes, iterates, replicates, and drives every automated task toward commodity pricing. AI cannot create in the way humans create. It cannot bisociate across domains. It cannot feel the gap in a market that doesn't show up in data yet. It cannot have a conversation about mushroom logistics at dinner and suddenly see a solution to a corporate training problem.

Every hour you spend trying to beat competitors at their own game is an hour you could spend creating a game they haven't seen yet. The skill stack from the last chapter is how you build the creative advantage. The Collision Method is how you exercise it. And Wattles, writing 115 years ago in language that sounds like a Victorian sermon, was pointing at exactly this: stop fighting over the same pie and go bake a new one.

The financial application is direct: competing on price is a race to the bottom. Competing on unique value, the value that only your specific skill stack and creative perspective can produce, is a race to a market of one. In a market of one, you set the price.

* * *

Let me tell you about a creativity exercise I've used weekly for over two years that has generated more genuinely original ideas than any brainstorming session I've ever sat through. I call it The Collision Method, and it is aggressively, deliberately stupid in its simplicity.

Take two random, unrelated topics. Force yourself to find ten connections between them. Not good connections. Not realistic connections. Any connections. The weirder, the better. The point isn't to produce viable business ideas (though that occasionally happens). The point is to train the pattern-recognition muscle that makes bisociation automatic.

Last month I collided "veterinary medicine" with "subscription box business model." Most of the connections were nonsense. But one of them, a subscription service that sends pet owners monthly behavioral enrichment activities designed by veterinary behaviorists, actually solved a real problem in a way I hadn't seen on the market. I'm not building that business. But the exercise produced an idea that someone should.

The financial value of this practice is indirect but enormous. The person who can see connections that others miss is the person who identifies market opportunities before they're obvious. That's the person who builds the business that the competition doesn't see coming. That's the person whose skill stack (Chapter 4) becomes more valuable because their imagination multiplies the value of everything else they know.

* * *

One uncomfortable truth before the exercise: most adults have had their creativity systematically suppressed.

George Land, a researcher who designed creativity tests for NASA, gave his assessment to 1,600 children at ages 5, 10, and 15. At five, 98% scored at the "creative genius" level. At ten, 30%. At fifteen, 12%. The same test given to adults? Two percent.

We don't lose creativity. We have it educated out of us by twelve years of being told to find the one right answer, follow the rubric, color inside the lines, and stop daydreaming. The capacity is still there. The neural architecture survived. It's just been buried under decades of convergent thinking training.

The exercises in this chapter aren't cute productivity tricks. They're rehabilitation for a cognitive ability that was actively suppressed. You were a creative genius at five. The wiring is still there. You just need to start using it again.

* * *

The Collision Method: This Week's Challenge

Do this once this week. It takes 20 minutes. It will feel pointless the first time. Do it anyway. Pointlessness is the feeling of your brain encountering unfamiliar cognitive terrain, and that's exactly where new pathways get built.

Open a random Wikipedia article (there's a "Random Article" button; use it). Write down the topic. Open a second random article. Write that topic down.

Set a timer for 15 minutes. Generate at least ten connections, products, services, or ideas that combine both topics. No filtering. No quality control. The critical rule: you are not allowed to say "these have nothing in common" and stop. That's the resistance. Push through it. The connections that feel most forced often produce the most surprising results.

When the timer ends, circle the one idea that surprises you most. Not the best one. The most surprising one. Surprise is the signature of genuine creativity.

Spend five more minutes developing it. What would it look like? Who would use it? What problem does it solve? What would you charge? You're not committing to building anything. You're training the muscle that sees opportunities where others see unrelated noise.

Do this weekly. Keep a log. Within two months, you'll notice something shifting: you'll start making connections involuntarily, in conversations, in meetings, while reading the news. That's the bisociation engine coming online. That's your imagination waking back up after years of being told to sit down and follow the rubric.

Hill told you imagination is the workshop of the mind. I'm telling you the workshop has been boarded up since middle school, and it's time to kick the door in.

CHAPTER 6

Organized Planning: Systems Beat Goals Every Time

Hill's Principle: "Crystallize desire into action through organized planning."

I once wrote a 47-page business plan for a venture that lasted four months.

Forty-seven pages. Financial projections for five years. Market analysis with charts. Competitive landscape with a SWOT matrix. Executive summary. Appendices. It was, objectively, a beautiful document. It was also fiction. Expensive, well-formatted fiction that bore almost no resemblance to what actually happened when the business met reality.

The customers I projected didn't materialize. The revenue model I designed didn't work. The timeline I planned was off by a factor of three. Every single assumption I'd baked into those 47 pages turned out to be either wrong or irrelevant. The only accurate part of the plan was the page numbers.

I tell you this not because planning is useless. Planning is essential. I tell you this because the kind of planning most people do, the detailed, rigid, assumption-heavy, five-year roadmap kind, is the wrong kind for the world we live in. It mistakes certainty for preparation. It confuses the elegance of the document with the quality of the strategy. And it gives you a very professional-looking map of a country that doesn't exist.

Hill's sixth principle is organized planning, and his instinct is right: desire without a plan is a wish, and the quality of the plan determines the quality of the outcome. But the planning model he described, and the one most people still use, was designed for a world where careers lasted 40 years and industries moved slowly enough for five-year projections to mean something. That world is gone.

* * *

The most important planning insight I've encountered comes from Scott Adams: goals are for losers; systems are for winners.

Before you assume he's being nihilistic, here's what he means. A goal is a specific outcome: lose 20 pounds, save $50,000, launch a business by June. A system is a recurring behavior that increases your odds across multiple outcomes: exercise every morning, invest 15% of every paycheck, spend two hours daily on your highest-leverage task.

The psychological difference is transformative. When you have a goal, you exist in a state of continuous failure until you achieve it. Every day between setting the goal and hitting it, your brain registers the gap. That gap creates a psychological drain that, over months, erodes motivation.

When you have a system, you succeed every time you execute. You invested this paycheck? Win. You did your two-hour deep work block? Win. You sent three outreach emails? Win. Every execution is a small victory, and small victories compound into large outcomes, often surpassing whatever arbitrary goal you would have set.

James Clear distilled this perfectly: you don't rise to the level of your goals; you fall to the level of your systems.

Let me make it concrete. Two people want to build a freelance consulting practice that generates $120,000 per year.

Person A plans backward: "I need $10,000 per month, so I need X clients at Y rate, which means Z proposals per week." This is clean, logical, and brittle. The moment reality deviates (and it always does), Person A has no adaptive mechanism. The plan assumed linearity in a nonlinear world.

Person B designs a system: "Every weekday, I spend 90 minutes on client outreach, 90 minutes on delivery, and 30 minutes on skill development. I track my close rate weekly and adjust my approach monthly." Person B doesn't have a fixed plan. Person B has a process that self-corrects. The system contains its own learning loop.

In my experience, working with people who build things for a living, Person B consistently outperforms Person A. Not because Person B wants it more. Because Person B built a machine instead of describing a destination.

* * *

I'm not anti-goal. Goals serve a purpose: they set direction. Without a direction, a system is just activity. The problem is when the goal becomes an idol and the system becomes an afterthought.

The OKR framework, developed by Andy Grove at Intel and later adopted by Google, Amazon, and most of Silicon Valley, reconciles goals and systems elegantly. An Objective is a qualitative, inspiring direction. Key Results are three to five quantitative measures that tell you whether you're making progress.

Objective: Build a sustainable freelance consulting business.

Key Result 1: Close four new clients this quarter.

Key Result 2: Achieve 80% client retention.

Key Result 3: Maintain a personal savings rate of 20% of gross revenue.

The Objective provides direction. The Key Results provide measurement. The system is whatever daily behaviors you design to move those Key Results. And critically, OKRs are set quarterly, not annually. John Doerr, who brought OKRs to Google, argues in Measure What Matters that quarterly cycles create urgency without false precision. Nobody can predict what they'll be doing in 11 months. But 90 days? Ninety days is real. Ninety days is a commitment you can actually honor.

I've used OKRs for my personal financial goals for three years. The format forces a discipline that vague annual resolutions never do. It's hard to lie to yourself when you've committed to three specific numbers and review them every 13 weeks. The numbers either moved or they didn't. The system either worked or it needs adjustment. There's no room for the comfortable fiction of "I'm making progress" when the Key Results say otherwise.

* * *

Modern planning requires something else Hill's generation didn't need: planning for a career that doesn't have a single path.

The average American changes jobs every four years. Entire industries appear and disappear within a decade. Skills that commanded premium compensation five years ago are being automated today. Planning in this environment demands a fundamentally different architecture.

Eric Ries, in The Lean Startup, gave us the framework: instead of perfecting a plan before launching, launch the simplest possible version, get real feedback, and iterate. Build-measure-learn. Fast cycles. Small bets. Constant adjustment. The planning happens in rapid loops, not in one grand upfront blueprint.

This applies to careers and personal finance as directly as it applies to startups. Instead of a five-year career plan, run a 90-day experiment. Instead of betting everything on one path, test two or three small hypotheses simultaneously. Instead of perfecting your business plan in a document, test your core assumption in the real world with real customers as fast as possible. If the assumption is wrong (and it usually is), you want to find out when you've invested $500, not $50,000.

* * *

Let me talk about what I call the Revenue Architecture, because organized planning in the modern economy means planning for more than one income source.

The belief that you should have one job providing all your income is a relic of the industrial era, and clinging to it is one of the riskiest financial positions you can hold. A single income stream means a single point of failure.

Layer one: Foundation Income. Your primary job or client base. It pays the bills. It provides stability. It doesn't need to be exciting. It needs to be reliable. This is the layer most people have. It's necessary. It's not sufficient.

Layer two: Growth Income. The project you're building with sweat equity. A side business, freelance work, a product in development. It's smaller than your Foundation Income but has higher ceiling potential. This is where you're investing today for tomorrow's options.

Layer three: Passive Income. Investment returns, royalties, digital products, rental income. This layer starts small. Painfully small. But it compounds, and eventually it's the layer that buys your freedom.

Layer four: Insurance Income. The emergency skill. The fallback you could monetize within a week if everything else collapsed. Tutoring, consulting, a trade skill, temp work in your field. It's not glamorous. It's a parachute. And parachutes don't need to be glamorous. They need to open.

When I audit my own Revenue Architecture, I can see exactly where I'm strong and where I'm exposed. My Foundation and Growth layers are solid. My Passive layer is underdeveloped relative to where I want it. That clarity, the ability to see the portfolio of income sources and identify the weak layer, is itself a product of organized planning. Without the framework, I'd just have a vague sense that "I should probably diversify my income." With the framework, I know exactly which layer to invest in this quarter.

* * *

One more planning tool that most books skip, and the one I wish someone had forced me to use fifteen years ago: the Pre-Mortem. It is the closest thing in this book to a cheat code, and like all cheat codes, you have to actually use it.

Developed by research psychologist Gary Klein, the Pre-Mortem is the deliberate inverse of visualization. Before you launch a plan, you don't imagine it succeeding. You imagine it has already failed, completely, irreversibly, humiliatingly, and then you work backward: *why* did it fail?

Not enough customers. Wrong pricing. Underestimated the time commitment. A competitor launched two months before you and captured the market you planned to enter. You burned out. Ran out of cash in month four. Your key partner quit. The technology you'd built on changed. Your spouse was right, and you should have listened at the kitchen table in March.

Most people experience these failure modes as unpleasant surprises. The Pre-Mortem turns them into inputs. You find them before they find you, while you can still do something about them, which is the entire point.

The Pre-Mortem Protocol

Here is the sequence I run on every significant financial commitment before I make it. Four steps. It takes 30 to 45 minutes. It has saved me more money than any planning exercise I know, and that is not me being dramatic for the dust jacket.

Step 1: Project the failure specifically. Do not write "it didn't work." Write the narrative. "We ran out of operating cash in month five because client acquisition cost was three times the estimate and our initial conversion rate was 12%, not the 28% we projected." The more specific the failure, the more useful the exercise. Vague failure modes produce vague contingencies. Specific failure modes produce actionable ones.

Step 2: Generate at least ten failure modes without filtering. This is the hardest part for optimistic people, which is most people who start businesses. Your brain will resist producing the tenth failure mode because it starts to feel like sabotage. Push through the resistance. Failure modes 8, 9, and 10 are usually the ones that actually happen. They are the scenarios your enthusiasm suppressed first, which is exactly why they were free to ambush you later.

Step 3: Categorize by probability and impact. Not every failure mode matters equally. Rate each one: how likely is it, and how bad would it be if it occurred? What you're looking for is the top-right quadrant: high probability, high impact. Those are not "risks to monitor." Those are threats to address before you launch.

Step 4: For the top three, write a specific contingency into the plan now. Not a vague note to "keep an eye on it." A concrete action, a decision rule, or a structural safeguard baked directly into your 90-Day Sprint. If "cash runs out in month four" is a top-three failure mode, your plan should include a specific cash threshold that triggers a predetermined pivot, before you're emotionally compromised by the situation. Future You, panicking at month four, is not the person you want making that call.

What It Actually Looks Like

Let me show you what the protocol produced when a client of mine, Marcus Chen, applied it to a real estate investment that looked, on paper, like one of the better opportunities he'd evaluated.

The property was a short-term rental in a coastal market. The spreadsheet was clean: projected occupancy at 72%, seasonal rate differentials accounted for, mortgage covered by revenue with a margin. His realtor was enthusiastic. His gut said yes.

Before he signed, Marcus ran the Pre-Mortem. Reluctantly. Like flossing.

Failure mode 1: *Seasonal cash flow volatility collapses the margin.* The market ran hot from May through September and cold from October through March. The spreadsheet showed annual averages. But averages don't pay the mortgage in November. When Marcus modeled month-by-month cash flow instead of annual totals, the winter gap required a five-month cash reserve just to break even in the off-season. He hadn't budgeted for that reserve. Severity: High. Probability: Certain.

Failure mode 2: *A regulatory change eliminates short-term rental permits.* A state bill restricting short-term rental licenses in tourist markets had quietly passed committee and was moving toward a floor vote. The bill had roughly even odds of passing, and if it did, the investment thesis dissolved. Marcus hadn't known the bill existed. A 20-minute search during the Pre-Mortem surfaced it.

Failure mode 3: *Dependency on a single contractor breaks the management model.* The entire operational plan hinged on one local property manager, a referral from the realtor who was selling him the property. No backup relationship. No contract. A person who could raise their rates or stop returning calls the month after closing. (You see the problem.)

None of those risks were visible in the spreadsheet. All three appeared within the first 15 minutes of the Pre-Mortem. Marcus walked away from the investment. Two years later, the short-term rental bill passed. The market he'd been looking at took a significant occupancy hit. The five-month cash reserve he hadn't planned for would have left him underwater regardless.

That Pre-Mortem was the highest-return 45 minutes Marcus has ever spent. He still buys me coffee about it.

The Optimism Objection

Someone, somewhere in the audience, is now wondering whether this is just pessimism wearing a productivity costume.

It isn't. And the distinction matters enough to address directly.

Pessimism assumes the outcome will be bad and stops there, usually with a beer. The Pre-Mortem assumes the outcome *could* be bad, identifies *why*, and then designs against those reasons. It doesn't counsel you not to jump. It tells you where the rocks are before you do. The entrepreneur who runs a Pre-Mortem and still launches is more prepared, not less optimistic. They're the person who packed a first aid kit before the hike, not the person who refused to hike.

The research on this is consistent. Gary Klein's own studies show that Pre-Mortem teams surface roughly 30% more potential problems than teams that don't conduct them, without any reduction in the team's willingness to proceed with sound plans. It filters bad bets more effectively than discussion does, because it bypasses the social pressure to be a team player and the cognitive bias toward confirming a decision already emotionally made.

Engineers build bridges to handle twice the expected load. Surgeons run pre-operative checklists. Airline pilots use pre-flight protocols before every single departure regardless of experience. Your financial plans deserve the same structural honesty. The Pre-Mortem is not a vote against your idea. It's the quality control system your idea deserves, and frankly, it loves you for it.

The AI Pre-Mortem Partner

One practical application worth naming directly: an AI language model makes an unusually effective Pre-Mortem partner, for a specific and counterintuitive reason. It has no emotional investment in your plan's success. It also has no kids in school with your kids.

When you run the Pre-Mortem with collaborators or advisors, there's always a social friction that softens the exercise. People don't want to be the one who's excessively negative. They pull their punches. They skip failure modes that feel impolite to name. ("Actually, I think your wife might leave" is hard to say across a conference table.)

An AI has none of those instincts. You can paste your plan into a capable model and prompt it:

"Assume this plan has failed completely within twelve months. Give me the fifteen most likely reasons it failed, ordered by probability. Be adversarial. Don't soften anything." It will return a list that includes failure modes your confirmation bias has suppressed and your colleagues were too polite to name.

The caveat: AI doesn't know your specific market, your relationships, your operational capacity, or the particular contractor whose reliability you're betting on. Its failure modes will be generic until you make the prompt specific. The more context you provide, meaning actual numbers, actual dependencies, actual market conditions, the more precisely the output targets your real vulnerabilities rather than statistical ones.

Use the AI output as a starting list. Add your own specific knowledge. Run Steps 3 and 4 yourself. The AI opens the exercise; your judgment closes it.

* * *

The CENTS Filter

MJ DeMarco, in The Millionaire Fastlane, created one of the most useful filters for evaluating whether a business can actually build wealth: CENTS. Control, Entry barriers, Need, Time-independence, and Scale.

Control: do you control the key variables? If your income depends entirely on a platform you don't own (Amazon, YouTube, someone else's marketplace), you don't have a business. You have a job that can be terminated by an algorithm change. I learned this lesson when a client who represented 40% of my freelance income disappeared after a reorganization. Overnight, my "business" lost nearly half its revenue because I'd built on someone else's foundation.

Entry barriers: how easy is it for someone to replicate what you're doing? If anyone with a laptop can do it, the market will flood and margins will collapse. Your skill stack is an entry barrier. Your specific expertise is an entry barrier. A generic service that requires no specialized knowledge is not.

Need: does the business solve a genuine problem that people will pay to fix? Not a problem you think exists. A problem that people are actively spending money to solve right now. The gap between "this is a cool idea" and "people will pay for this" has killed more businesses than any recession.

Time-independence: can the business generate income without your direct, hour-by-hour involvement? If you must be present for every dollar earned, you've built a job, not a business. The difference between self-employment and business ownership is leverage: can the machine run without you in the room?

Scale: can the business serve 10x more customers without 10x more effort? A one-on-one service is valuable but not scalable. A digital product, a software platform, a content library, a licensing model, these can grow without proportional increases in labor.

Run every business idea through CENTS before you invest serious time or money. If it fails three or more of the five criteria, it might generate income, but it's unlikely to build wealth. I now apply this filter reflexively, and it has saved me from at least three ventures that sounded exciting but had fatal structural flaws.

* * *

Fear-Setting: The Pre-Mortem's Cousin

The Pre-Mortem and Fear-Setting are often confused because they sound like variations on the same anxiety.

They're not.

The Pre-Mortem is a *plan* stress-test: it interrogates the structural vulnerabilities of a specific system or venture before you launch it. Fear-Setting is a *personal* risk calibration: it interrogates your own psychological readiness to act under uncertainty.

You use the Pre-Mortem to find the cracks in the bridge. You use Fear-Setting to decide whether you're willing to cross it anyway. Both exercises are necessary. Neither replaces the other. And the order matters: Pre-Mortem first, so you know what you're actually afraid of. Fear-Setting second, so you know whether the fear is proportionate.

Tim Ferriss introduced a practice called Fear-Setting that complements the Pre-Mortem beautifully. Where the Pre-Mortem asks "why might this fail?" Fear-Setting asks "what's the absolute worst that could happen, and could I survive it?"

The exercise has three columns. Column one: Define the worst-case scenario in specific, concrete detail. Not vague dread. Specifics. "I invest $5,000 and the business fails. I lose the $5,000. I have to go back to freelancing full-time for six months to rebuild savings."

Column two: What could you do to prevent or minimize each scenario? "I start with $2,000 instead of $5,000. I keep my freelance clients during the experiment. I set a 90-day Kill Criteria."

Column three: What could you do to repair the damage if the worst case happened? "I have an emergency fund. I have marketable skills. I could find freelance work within two weeks."

Most people discover that the worst case, when made specific, is survivable and reversible. The fear was bigger than the reality. And the cost of inaction, which Ferriss calls the "atrocity of the status quo," is usually higher than the cost of a failed experiment.

I've used Fear-Setting before every significant financial risk I've taken in the last five years. The consistent finding: the worst case is always less catastrophic than my anxiety suggested, and always more recoverable than my fear wanted me to believe.

* * *

The 90-Day Sprint: This Week's Challenge

This replaces the five-year plan. It takes about 45 minutes to build, and you'll rebuild it every 90 days. The first one is the hardest. After that, it becomes a rhythm.

Define one Objective for the next 90 days. One. Not five. The single most important thing you could accomplish that would move your financial life forward. Write it as a statement that makes you slightly nervous. If it doesn't make you nervous, it's not ambitious enough.

Define three Key Results that would prove you achieved the Objective. Specific. Measurable. Binary. You either hit them or you didn't. "Kind of" is not a measurement.

Design the daily system. What behaviors, executed consistently, give you the best shot at those Key Results? Be uncomfortably specific. "Work on my business" is not a system. "6 to 7:30 AM: send four outreach emails using Template B, then update the pipeline tracker" is a system.

Run a Pre-Mortem. Assume the sprint failed. Why? List every reason. For the three most likely, write a specific contingency into the plan right now.

Assess your Revenue Architecture. Which layers do you have? Which are weak? Which are missing? What is one concrete action you can take this quarter to strengthen the weakest layer?

Schedule a weekly review. Fifteen minutes every Sunday. Are you executing the system? Are the Key Results moving? What needs adjustment? This is the learning loop that turns a static plan into a living system. Without it, your plan is a document. With it, your plan is an engine.

Hill told you to crystallize desire into action through organized planning. The upgrade: crystallize desire into a system, measure the system with Key Results, stress-test it with a Pre-Mortem, and iterate every 90 days. My 47-page business plan was a beautiful corpse. The 90-Day Sprint is a living thing. Build the living thing.

PART THREE

The Think Again Loop: Execute with Feedback

CHAPTER 7

Decision: Stop Overthinking, Start Choosing

Hill's Principle: "Procrastination, the opposite of decision, is a common enemy which practically every man must conquer."

What is the most expensive decision you didn't make last year?

Not the bad decision. Not the one you made and it went wrong. The one you avoided entirely. The raise you didn't ask for. The investment you researched for six months and never pulled the trigger on. The business you planned and replanned and refined and adjusted and never launched. The conversation about money with your spouse that you've been "waiting for the right time" to have for three years.

Indecision has a cost, and the cost is invisible, which makes it the most dangerous cost in your financial life. Bad decisions announce themselves: you lose money, you lose time, you get feedback. But the decisions you avoid? Those costs never show up on any statement. They exist only as the gap between what your life is and what it could have been, and that gap is unknowable, which makes it easy to pretend it isn't there.

Napoleon Hill observed that successful people make decisions quickly and change them slowly, while unsuccessful people make decisions slowly and change them quickly. He documented this pattern across hundreds of interviews, and it remains one of his sharpest observations. But he described the pattern without explaining the machinery behind it.

Why do smart, capable, well-informed people struggle to decide? And what can you actually do about it?

* * *

The machinery has a name: decision fatigue.

Roy Baumeister showed that every decision you make, from what to eat for breakfast to whether to invest in a rental property, draws from the same pool of cognitive resources. That pool is finite. It depletes throughout the day. And when it's depleted, you make bad decisions or you make no decisions at all.

This is why judges grant parole at significantly higher rates in the morning than in the afternoon. It's why you impulse-buy junk food at the grocery store at 7 PM but not at 7 AM. It's why Steve Jobs wore the same outfit every day and Obama limited his suits to two colors. They were conserving cognitive fuel for the decisions that actually moved the needle.

The financial implication is direct: if you're spending your decision-making energy on 50 trivial choices before noon, you have nothing left for the important ones. What to wear, what to eat, which route to drive, how to respond to 30 low-stakes emails: each one is a small withdrawal from a finite account. And the financial decisions, the ones that actually compound over decades, get whatever is left over. Usually that's fumes.

I learned this the hard way during a period when I was building a side business while working a full-time job. My best financial thinking happened at 6 AM, before the decision avalanche of the workday started. By evening, when I tried to work on the business, I was making terrible choices: impulsive purchases for the business, unfocused planning, agreeing to commitments I should have declined. I wasn't less motivated in the evening. I was less capable. The cognitive tank was empty.

The fix wasn't motivation. It was architecture. I moved all significant financial and business decisions to the morning. I automated or eliminated dozens of daily micro-decisions. Meal prep on Sunday. Same morning routine every day. Automated bill pay. Email templates for common responses. Each elimination freed cognitive resources for the decisions that actually built wealth.

* * *

Barry Schwartz added another layer to this problem. His research on choice demonstrates that having more options doesn't make you a better decision-maker. It makes you worse.

Schwartz identifies two types: satisficers, who set criteria and choose the first option that meets them, and maximizers, who search exhaustively for the absolute best option.

Maximizers consistently report lower satisfaction, more regret, and worse outcomes. Not because their choices are objectively worse, but because they spend so much time choosing that they lose the time, energy, and momentum they could have spent executing.

I am a recovering maximizer, and I can tell you exactly what that costs. I once spent three weeks researching project management apps for a new business venture. Three weeks. Comparison articles. YouTube reviews. Free trials of seven platforms. A spreadsheet with features, pricing, integrations. Two Reddit threads. (Never read the Reddit threads.) After three weeks, I chose Trello, spent another week customizing it, and realized I had done zero actual project management. The tool I was supposed to use to manage work had become the work, and the real work hadn't moved an inch.

That's maximizing in action. The pursuit of the optimal choice became a substitute for the thing the choice was supposed to enable. And the opportunity cost, three weeks of actual business-building, is invisible and permanent.

* * *

Jeff Bezos offers the most useful decision framework I've encountered. He categorizes decisions into two types.

Type 1 decisions are irreversible. One-way doors. Once through, you can't go back. These deserve careful analysis. Getting married. Signing a 30-year mortgage. Selling your company. Take your time.

Type 2 decisions are reversible. Two-way doors. If the choice doesn't work, you walk back through and try something else. The cost of being wrong is low and recoverable. Choosing a project management tool. Trying a new marketing channel. Hiring a contractor. Experimenting with a pricing model.

Bezos's insight: most decisions are Type 2, but most people treat them as Type 1. They bring the full weight of irreversible-decision anxiety to choices that could easily be reversed. They agonize over two-way doors as if their life depended on getting the handle right.

His rule: for Type 2 decisions, decide with about 70% of the information you wish you had. At 70%, you know enough to be reasonable. If you're wrong, you course-correct. If you wait for 90%, you're almost always too slow, and the cost of delay exceeds the cost of being slightly wrong.

I now explicitly classify every significant decision before I make it. Is this a one-way door or a two-way door? If it's two-way, I set a 48-hour maximum deliberation period and decide at the end regardless of whether I feel ready. The decisions aren't always perfect. But the velocity is transformative. While my competitors are still researching, I'm on my second iteration.

* * *

John Boyd, a fighter pilot who revolutionized military strategy, developed a concept called the OODA loop: Observe, Orient, Decide, Act. His argument was that the side that cycles through this loop faster wins. Not because every decision is right, but because faster iteration means faster learning, and faster learning converges on the right answer before the slow side finishes deliberating.

Boyd proved this empirically. The American F-86 Sabre had worse technical specs than the Soviet MiG-15 in Korea. But the F-86 had a bubble canopy for better visibility and hydraulic controls for faster response. American pilots could observe and orient faster, so they decided and acted faster. Their OODA loop was tighter. The kill ratio was 10 to 1.

The parallel to business and wealth-building is direct: the speed at which you learn matters more than the quality of any single decision. Decide quickly. Observe the result. Orient to the new data. Decide again. Each cycle makes the next decision better, and the compound effect of fast iteration is an insurmountable advantage over time.

* * *

AI decision-support tools are proliferating, and the temptation to outsource decisions to them is real. Before you do, it's worth understanding exactly what you're outsourcing.

There is a useful distinction between AI-assisted decisions and AI-delegated ones.

Assisted: you use AI to surface options, stress-test your reasoning, model scenarios, and flag blind spots you haven't considered. Then *you* decide. This is legitimate, often excellent, and consistent with everything the OODA Loop argues. AI accelerates your observe and orient phases, which tightens your loop.

Delegated: you let the AI make the call. For Type 2 decisions, the low-stakes, reversible, data-rich kind, this can be reasonable. For any decision involving values, relationships, irreversibility, or the question of who you want to become, this is a category error. AI will give you a confident answer. It will not be able to tell you what the decision means, because meaning requires a life it hasn't lived. The model has not buried a parent. The model has not held a hand at a hospital bedside. Keep that in mind before you ask it whether to leave your marriage.

The rule: use AI to think faster. Make decisions yourself. And verify that your AI prompt reflects your actual values, not a simplified version of them.

* * *

Steven Levitt, of Freakonomics, ran a study that should permanently cure anyone's fear of making the wrong Type 2 decision. He set up a website where people who were struggling with a decision could flip a virtual coin: heads, make the change; tails, maintain the status quo.

He followed up six months later. The result: people who got heads (and made the change) were significantly happier than people who got tails (and didn't), regardless of what the decision was. Quitting a job, ending a relationship, starting a business, moving to a new city: across categories, action beat inaction.

The content of the decision mattered less than the act of deciding. The people who made a change were happier because they had agency. They had moved. They had information. They were somewhere new, even if somewhere new wasn't perfect.

The people who didn't decide? They were still sitting in the same uncertainty, burning cognitive energy on the same unresolved question, six months later.

Indecision is not caution. Indecision is a slow leak in your cognitive fuel tank, and it drains resources you could be spending on execution, learning, and iteration.

* * *

A note specifically for smart, educated people, because intelligence creates its own decision-making trap.

If you're intelligent, you're very good at generating reasons not to act. For any potential decision, you can identify 17 risks, 12 downsides, 9 alternative approaches, and 4 catastrophic scenarios. You can argue both sides with equal conviction. All of this cognitive firepower, instead of helping you decide, paralyzes you.

The antidote is decision rules: pre-commitments that bypass analysis when you recognize you're in a Type 2 situation.

"If an opportunity costs less than $500 and has upside potential, I try it without further analysis." "If I've been deliberating more than 48 hours on a reversible decision, I choose the option that scares me slightly more." "If my gut says yes and my spreadsheet says maybe, I go with my gut for Type 2."

These sound simplistic. That's the point. They exist to override the complexity engine that smart people run on everything, including things that don't deserve that much processing power.

* * *

The Decision Diet: This Week's Challenge

Seven days. Three phases. One overdue decision.

Phase one (Day 1-2): Track and categorize. Write down every decision you make on Day 1, from morning to night. It will be a shockingly long list.

Day 2, categorize each as High Impact (moves your financial or professional life forward) or Low Impact. Count the ratio. For most people, it's about 95% Low Impact.

Phase two (Days 3-5): Eliminate five. Pick five Low Impact decisions and automate, eliminate, or batch them. Plan meals on Sunday. Set out clothes the night before. Auto-pay every bill. Create email templates. Batch errands into one trip. Each elimination is a deposit into your cognitive account for the decisions that actually matter.

Phase three (Days 6-7): The Big One. Identify the decision you've been avoiding. The one sitting in the back of your mind consuming energy like a background app draining your battery.

Write it down. Classify it: Type 1 or Type 2. If it's Type 2, you have until end of Day 7 to decide. Not a perfect decision. A decision. If it's Type 1, schedule a 60-minute focused session with a trusted advisor within two weeks to analyze it properly.

Notice how you feel on Day 7 after deciding. Most people report a specific physical sensation: a lightness, a release of tension they didn't realize they were carrying. That's the cognitive weight of indecision leaving your body. It was there the whole time, taxing you, and you'd stopped noticing it the same way you stop noticing a heavy backpack until someone takes it off.

Hill said the world rewards decisiveness. He was right, but the reason isn't mystical. The reason is that decisions free cognitive resources, create learning opportunities through feedback, and generate momentum that compounds over time.

Every decision you avoid is a tax on every other decision you make.

Stop paying the tax. Start choosing.

CHAPTER 8

Persistence: Grit, Quit, or Pivot?

Hill's Principle: "Persistence is the sustained effort necessary to induce faith."

I need to tell you about a Tuesday in 2019 when I sat in my car in a parking lot for 45 minutes trying to decide whether to quit something I'd been building for two years.

I won't bore you with the specifics. What matters is that I'd invested significant time, meaningful money, and a large piece of my identity into this project. It was supposed to be the thing. The vehicle. The proof that I could build something real. And after two years of consistent effort, honest execution, and genuinely good work, the key metric was flat. Not declining. Not growing. Flat. The trend line looked like the horizon.

And I could feel two competing voices in my head, both absolutely certain they were right.

Voice one said: You're three feet from gold. Every great success story has a chapter where the founder almost quit. This is that chapter. Push through. The breakthrough is coming. Don't be the cautionary tale who gave up too soon.

Voice two said: You're three feet from a sewer line. The data is clear. The trend is flat. Continuing to invest in something that isn't working isn't persistence. It's ego maintenance. Walk away, redirect the resources, and build something that actually has evidence of working.

Both voices quoted Napoleon Hill. Both were persuasive. And sitting in that parking lot, I realized that Hill's chapter on persistence, for all its emotional power, had left me completely unequipped to tell the difference between productive persistence and expensive stubbornness. He told me never to quit. He didn't tell me how to know when quitting is the smartest thing I could do.

* * *

Hill's most famous persistence story is the man who stopped digging three feet from a massive gold vein. The moral is clear and intoxicating: don't quit, because your breakthrough might be just beyond where you stopped.

It's a beautiful parable. It's also a selection bias wrapped in a motivational blanket. For every person who was three feet from gold, there are hundreds who were three feet from nothing and kept digging because a book told them quitters are losers. We just don't hear their stories, because "I persisted and it still didn't work" doesn't sell tickets to motivational seminars.

Behavioral economists call this the sunk cost fallacy: the tendency to continue investing in something because of what you've already invested, rather than based on future expected returns. You've spent $20,000 and two years on a business that isn't working. Rational analysis says it's unlikely to succeed. But your brain says, "I can't walk away now. I've already put in too much."

The $20,000 and the two years are gone regardless of what you do next. They're sunk. They are as relevant to your future decision as the weather in 1987. The only thing that matters is: given what I know now, is further investment likely to produce a return? If the answer is no, every additional dollar and hour is a new loss, not a recovery of old ones.

* * *

Angela Duckworth's research on grit is real, replicated, and important. Sustained passion and effort toward long-term goals is a stronger predictor of success than IQ, talent, or socioeconomic background. Hill was right that persistence matters.

But Duckworth herself has been careful to note what the pop-culture version of her work ignores: grit is about persisting toward the right goal. Grit applied to the wrong thing is just a very determined person walking into a wall. Faster. With more conviction. Into the same wall.

Annie Duke, in Quit: The Power of Knowing When to Walk Away, addresses this gap directly. Duke, a former professional poker player, points out that the best poker players fold most of their hands. Folding isn't failure. It's resource management. Recognizing that this particular hand doesn't justify the bet and redeploying your chips toward a better opportunity.

Every hour, dollar, and unit of energy you spend persisting on a losing venture is an hour, dollar, and unit of energy unavailable for a winning one. Persistence has an opportunity cost, and nobody talks about it because "never give up" fits on a t-shirt and "strategically reallocate resources based on updated probability assessments" does not.

* * *

So how do you actually tell the difference? I've developed three frameworks that I use, and the first one has to be implemented before you start, not after you're already emotionally invested.

Framework one: Kill Criteria.

Before you begin any venture, define the specific, measurable conditions under which you will walk away. Not during the venture, when sunk costs are screaming and your ego is negotiating. Before. When you're rational.

"If monthly recurring revenue hasn't reached $2,000 within 12 months, I will pivot or shut down." "If customer acquisition cost exceeds $50 after 6 months of optimization, this model isn't viable." "If I'm working 70-hour weeks with no margin improvement after 18 months, this is a job, not a business."

Kill Criteria work because they're decisions made in advance by your rational self for your future emotional self. They're a contract with yourself, signed before the feelings get involved.

I now set Kill Criteria for every significant financial commitment. The real estate investment I didn't make (from the planning chapter's Pre-Mortem) also had Kill Criteria that would have triggered had I invested. The project I sat in the parking lot agonizing over? I didn't have Kill Criteria. I'd started it with pure enthusiasm and no exit conditions. That's why I ended up in a parking lot for 45 minutes instead of making a clean decision based on pre-agreed metrics.

Framework two: The Fresh Eyes Test.

Ask yourself: if I were starting from scratch today, knowing everything I now know, would I begin this? Not "should I continue." Would I begin?

This question cuts through sunk cost like a scalpel. It reframes the decision from "should I protect my investment" to "is this the best use of my resources going forward." The past is irrelevant. The only thing that matters is future expected value.

It's also the hardest question you'll ever ask yourself honestly, because your brain has spent months or years constructing a narrative about why this path is right, and the Fresh Eyes Test asks you to evaluate it as a stranger would. A stranger who has no ego invested, no identity attached, no story to protect. Just the facts, the data, and the question: would you start this today?

Framework three: Trend Analysis.

Don't evaluate based on a snapshot. Evaluate based on trajectory. Is the key metric improving, flat, or declining?

Improving, even slowly? Persistence is justified. You're on a curve. Optimize the rate, but stay.

Flat despite genuine effort? You have a system problem, not a persistence problem. Something in your approach isn't working, and more effort in the same direction won't fix it. This is where pivoting, changing the approach while keeping the goal, makes sense.

Declining despite your best work? That's the signal. Declining trends in a well-executed plan usually mean the premise is wrong. And grit doesn't fix a wrong premise.

My parking lot project? Flat trend. Six months of flat data after 18 months of effort. The Fresh Eyes Test was clear: I would not start this today. I pivoted. I redirected the time and energy into a project that showed early traction, and within eight months that project was generating more value than the flat one had generated in two years.

* * *

The pivot deserves its own discussion, because it's the missing third option between persist and quit, and it's where a surprising amount of wealth gets built.

A pivot isn't quitting. It's redirecting what you've learned toward a better opportunity. Slack started as an internal tool for a failing video game company. The game died. The communication tool they'd built for their team turned out to be the real product. Stewart Butterfield didn't quit or persist. He pivoted. And the pivot produced a company that sold for $27.7 billion.

Shopify started when Tobias Lutke tried to sell snowboards online and couldn't find decent e-commerce software. He built his own. The snowboard business was fine. The e-commerce platform was a $60 billion company. The pivot wasn't away from failure. It was toward the unexpected signal that emerged during execution.

Pivoting requires two things that pure grit doesn't: the humility to admit your original idea was wrong, and the awareness to notice what's actually working even when it's not what you planned. You can't see either of those if you're not tracking data. You can't see either if your identity is fused to the original plan.

* * *

Which brings me to identity, the deepest layer of the persistence problem.

When you've invested years in something, it becomes part of who you are. "I'm a startup founder." "I'm building a real estate portfolio." "I'm writing a novel." The venture stops being something you do and becomes something you are. And when something is part of your identity, quitting it feels like losing a piece of yourself.

The antidote is defining your identity at a higher level of abstraction. "I'm a restaurateur" is brittle. If the restaurant fails, you fail. "I'm someone who creates experiences that bring people together" is flexible. The restaurant can fail, and you can pivot to events, catering, community spaces, or something entirely new without an identity crisis.

My parking lot identity crisis resolved when I reframed. I wasn't abandoning the project. I was redirecting the skills, knowledge, and relationships I'd built toward a better vehicle. I wasn't a quitter. I was someone who builds things, and this particular thing was done. The next one was waiting.

That reframe took me about four months to fully internalize. It wasn't instant. Identity doesn't update like software. But it did update, and every update made the next pivot easier.

* * *

What I Built After the Parking Lot

I want to close the loop on my parking lot story, because the aftermath matters more than the crisis.

After I walked away from the two-year project, I spent about a month in what I can only describe as productive grief. I wasn't depressed. I was processing. I was letting go of the identity I'd attached to the venture and rebuilding my sense of professional self at a higher level of abstraction. Not "I'm building X." Instead: "I'm someone who builds things, and X is done."

During that month, I noticed something I'd been ignoring for the entire two years: a different opportunity had been growing quietly in the background. A skill I'd been developing as a side activity, almost a hobby, had been generating small but consistent positive signals. People were reaching out about it. The engagement metrics, which I'd been too focused on the main project to track, showed a clear upward trend.

I pivoted toward it. Within eight months, it was generating more value than the original project had in two years. Not because I was smarter. Because the signal was real, the trend was positive, and I was finally available to see it.

The lesson: the parking lot wasn't the end of the story. It was the plot twist. And the only reason the plot twist was possible is that I freed up the resources, time, energy, attention, and identity space to notice what was already working.

Annie Duke calls this "opportunity cost awareness." Every hour spent persisting on a flat trend is an hour unavailable for a rising one. The math of persistence isn't just about what you're persisting on. It's about what you're persisting away from.

AI can sharpen the data side of this decision: trend analysis, competitor benchmarking, market signal reading, financial projection modeling. Use it for those. What AI cannot do is tell you whether to quit, because that judgment requires knowing your values, your energy reserves, your opportunity cost in personal terms, and what this venture actually means to you. The Kill Criteria, the conditions under which you walk away, must be written by a human, because they encode human priorities. No model can weight those for you.

* * *

The Quit Criteria Checklist: This Week's Challenge

Do this for every active venture, project, or major financial commitment in your life. Twenty minutes each. It's cheap insurance against years of misallocated effort.

Define the venture in one sentence. If you can't describe it in one sentence, you might not understand it well enough to evaluate it.

Write three Kill Criteria. Specific, measurable, time-bound. The conditions under which you will walk away. Write them while you're calm. That's the whole point.

Apply the Fresh Eyes Test. If you were starting today with everything you now know, would you begin this? Write a paragraph. Be honest enough to make yourself uncomfortable.

Assess the trend. Pull whatever data you have on the key metric. Improving, flat, or declining? If flat or declining for more than 90 days, write a specific change to your approach (not your effort level, your approach) that you'll implement and measure over the next 30 days.

Check your identity. Write the identity statement you've attached to this venture. Then rewrite it one level higher. Find the version that survives a pivot. That's the version to hold.

Share this with someone who will tell you the truth. Not someone who will reassure you. Someone who will look at the data and give you an honest read. Ask them: "Based on this, should I persist, pivot, or quit?" Listen with the part of your brain that wants to learn, not the part that wants to be right.

Hill told you to never give up. That was incomplete. Persist when the evidence supports it. Pivot when the trend says your approach is wrong. Quit when the premise is broken. And never, ever let your ego make the decision.

The bravest financial decision I ever made was walking away from something I'd built for two years. It felt like failure for about a month. Then the resources I freed up went into something that actually worked, and the "failure" revealed itself to be a redirection that was worth every dollar and every hour I'd spent learning what didn't work.

That's not quitting. That's winning on a longer timeline than your ego is comfortable with.

CHAPTER 9

The Wealth Bridge: Money, Meaning, and Why You Need Both

A bridge chapter. No Hill principle. Just an honest conversation.

A few years ago, I hit a financial milestone I'd been targeting for a long time. I'd spent years thinking about that number, tracking progress, treating it as the finish line of a race I'd been running since my twenties.

When I crossed it, I felt absolutely nothing.

Not triumph. Not relief. Not the cinematic, slow-motion satisfaction the achievement was supposed to deliver. A mild internal "huh." A momentary recognition that the spreadsheet now said what I'd wanted it to say. And then a question that landed like a brick: now what?

I had optimized for a number without understanding what the number was for.

I'm pausing the principle march for this chapter because what I'm about to tell you is more important than any framework in this book. The principles work. They will help you build wealth. But wealth built without answering the question this chapter asks is a destination you'll arrive at only to discover you never decided where you actually wanted to go.

* * *

I want to tell you about the conversation that changed my financial life more than any book, any course, or any strategy ever did. It wasn't with a financial advisor. It wasn't at a seminar. It was with Izzy, on a Sunday afternoon, at our kitchen table.

She had been running her handywoman business for a while by then, and she'd had a week that was physically exhausting but deeply satisfying. She'd fixed a single mom's plumbing, rebuilt a porch railing for a retired couple, and installed a ceiling fan for a family who'd been living without air circulation in a Florida July. She was tired and she was happy, and she said something offhand that I've thought about almost every day since: "I don't need more work. I need the right amount of the right work."

The right amount of the right work.

I was sitting there with a spreadsheet open on my laptop, chasing a number I'd never interrogated, and my wife, who doesn't have an MBA and has never read a single wealth-building book, had articulated in one sentence the thing that every financial optimization model I'd ever built was missing. The question wasn't how much. The question was what for.

That conversation led to an exercise I'll give you at the end of this chapter. But first, let me tell you what we discovered when we actually did it, because the specifics matter more than the concept.

* * *

We sat down on a different Sunday and described our ideal ordinary Tuesday. Not a vacation. Not a special occasion. Just a regular Tuesday in the life we actually wanted.

My version: wake up without an alarm around 7. Coffee on the porch while reading something unrelated to work. Two focused writing blocks in the morning. A workout around noon. Lunch that I actually cook instead of inhaling at my desk. An afternoon split between collaborative work and a project I'm building for myself. Dinner with Izzy. An evening with no screens, no obligations, and no guilt about either.

Izzy's version: wake up early. Two or three jobs scheduled for the morning, the kind that use her hands and leave visible results. Home by 2 PM. Time to ride her motorcycle or work on a personal project. Dinner together. Simple.

Neither of us described a mansion. Neither of us described a luxury car. Neither of us described the version of success that the internet insists we should want. Our ideal Tuesday was modest, specific, and centered on autonomy, creative work, and time together.

Then we costed it out.

Housing in Central Florida, at the standard we actually wanted, not the standard Instagram suggests we should want. Food at the level we described. Transportation. Healthcare. A reasonable discretionary budget. The annual total was about 40% lower than the number I'd been chasing.

Forty percent.

That means I'd been unconsciously planning to work years longer than necessary, pursuing a target that existed only because I'd never questioned where it came from. It came from comparison. It came from the ambient cultural pressure to want more without ever defining what more means. It came from the financial industry, which profits when the goalpost keeps moving because a moving goalpost is a customer for life.

Defining enough didn't make me less ambitious. It made me more focused. Instead of pouring energy into reaching a vague, inflated number, I could build specifically toward the life I actually wanted and redirect the surplus toward things that mattered: freedom, time, creative projects, and not grinding until my body gave out in service of a number that wouldn't have made me any happier than the lower one.

* * *

What is wealth actually for?

The financial industry cannot answer this question for you because the industry profits from never letting you answer it. You hit $100,000 and they say $500,000. You hit $500,000 and they say a million. The goalpost doesn't stop moving because a stationary goalpost is a satisfied customer, and satisfied customers stop buying financial products.

The research on money and happiness has been refined over decades. Daniel Kahneman and Angus Deaton's original finding, updated by Matthew Killingsworth in 2021, shows that emotional wellbeing increases with income up to roughly $75,000 to $100,000, after which the curve flattens substantially. Life satisfaction continues increasing beyond that, but at diminishing returns. The jump from $30,000 to $60,000 transforms daily life. The jump from $300,000 to $600,000 barely registers emotionally.

This doesn't mean money above $100,000 is meaningless. It means it operates differently. Below $100,000, money solves problems. Above $100,000, money buys options. The fulfillment comes not from the money itself but from how wisely you deploy those options.

Morgan Housel tells the story of Rajat Gupta, former managing director of McKinsey, worth $100 million, who committed insider trading because he wanted to be a billionaire. He had enough by any rational standard. But the concept of enough had never been defined, and the undefined goalpost led him to a federal prison. The same dynamic plays out at every income level, less dramatically but just as destructively.

This is also where AI financial tools most clearly show their limits.

An AI can calculate your freedom number. It can model your savings trajectory, project compound returns, and estimate when your investment income exceeds your expenses. What it cannot do is tell you what your ideal ordinary Tuesday looks like, because that information doesn't exist in any database. It lives in you. The algorithm that has been tracking your behavior, your clicks, your purchases, and your aspirational content for the last decade will give you a number, sure. That number will be calibrated to what people with your demographic profile typically want, not what *you* actually want when you sit still long enough to ask. The model is solving a different equation than the one you live in.

The Enough Exercise at the end of this chapter is the thing AI cannot do for you. Do it yourself. Pen, paper, quiet room. The old technology still works.

* * *

FIRE stands for Financial Independence, Retire Early.

The movement has deeper roots than most people realize: Vicki Robin and Joe Dominguez laid the philosophical groundwork in *Your Money or Your Life* in 1992, framing money as life-energy traded for dollars rather than as an end in itself.

The internet turned those ideas into a community in the early 2000s, with bloggers like Mr. Money Mustache building devoted followings around one central premise: that aggressive saving and investing could compress a forty-year working life into ten or fifteen years, regardless of income.

By the mid-2010s, FIRE had migrated from the fringe to feature articles in the *New York Times* and *Wall Street Journal*, and a generation of readers who were skeptical of the traditional retirement timeline had a name, a framework, and a spreadsheet for what they were already quietly building toward.

The FIRE movement introduced a useful concept: the crossover point, the moment when investment income exceeds living expenses. After that, work is optional. At its best, FIRE isn't about retirement. It's about choosing whether to work, which is the most valuable thing money can buy.

At its worst, FIRE becomes its own prison: people sacrificing every present experience for a future that may not arrive, defining identity through a savings rate instead of a life.

Vicki Robin reframed this beautifully: every dollar represents hours of your life traded for it. When your effective hourly wage is $20, a $200 gadget costs ten hours. Not $200. Ten hours of the only non-renewable resource you have.

I started evaluating purchases this way after the kitchen table conversation. A $15 lunch? Less than an hour of life-energy. Fine. A $300 gadget I'll use twice? Fifteen hours for something that ends up in a drawer. The math makes some decisions effortless and others impossible to justify.

* * *

Most wealth books skip lifestyle design entirely, which is like building a rocket without choosing a destination.

The standard approach: accumulate money, then figure out what to do with your life. The better approach: figure out what you want your daily life to look like, then engineer the financial structure to support it.

The life you actually want is almost always cheaper than the life you think you should want. The comparison-driven, status-signaling version is extraordinarily expensive. The version built around your actual values? Often surprisingly affordable.

I know people earning $400,000 who are miserable because their lifestyle costs $410,000. I know people earning $85,000 who are thriving because their lifestyle costs $60,000 and the surplus is buying them freedom. The first group looks wealthier. The second group is wealthier by the only definition that matters: the gap between what they have and what they need.

* * *

There's an uncomfortable truth in this chapter that I need to say directly, from personal experience: some people use the pursuit of wealth to avoid dealing with the parts of their life that are actually broken.

If your marriage is struggling, it's easier to pour yourself into the business. If you're lonely, it's easier to chase a number than to do the vulnerable work of building relationships. If you're grieving or anxious, the pursuit of more money provides a socially acceptable way to never sit still with your feelings.

I've done this. I've used work as an escape from emotional discomfort and told myself it was ambition. The work felt productive. The feelings felt dangerous. So I chose productive and called it discipline.

I've watched people reach their financial goals and discover that the hole they were filling was never money-shaped. It was meaning-shaped. Connection-shaped. Purpose-shaped. No amount of zeros fills a hole shaped like something else.

The kitchen table conversation with Izzy wasn't just about a number. It was about stopping long enough to ask what the numbers were in service of. And the answer, once we sat with it honestly, was simpler, cheaper, and more achievable than anything I'd been chasing.

That might be the most valuable financial insight I've ever had. It didn't come from a book. It came from sitting still long enough to listen.

* * *

Dreamlining vs. Goal-Setting

Tim Ferriss introduced an exercise called Dreamlining that is essentially what you just did with the ideal Tuesday exercise, but with a sharper edge. Ferriss's version asks three questions: What would you do if you couldn't fail? What would you have? What would you be? Then he forces you to calculate the monthly cost of each answer.

The Dreamlining insight that hit me hardest: most people's dreams cost far less than they assume. The fantasy of "being rich" feels expensive because it's vague. The reality of the specific life you want, once priced, is often achievable on a timeline that's measured in years, not decades.

Where Dreamlining goes further than a standard goal-setting exercise is in the timeline pressure. Ferriss argues that a six-month dream is more motivating and more achievable than a ten-year dream, because short timelines force creative problem-solving while long timelines enable procrastination. You can't "wait and see" when the deadline is 26 weeks away.

I've combined the ideal Tuesday exercise with Dreamlining's timeline pressure. The question isn't just "what does enough look like" but "what's the shortest credible path from here to there?" The answer is always shorter than you think when you strip away the status markers you were unconsciously including.

* * *

The Enough Exercise: This Week's Challenge

This is the most important exercise in the book. Everything else is tactics. This is strategy. The kitchen table conversation that changed my life took about 90 minutes. Yours might take less. Do it with a partner if you have one. Do it alone if you don't. But do it.

Describe your ideal ordinary Tuesday in detail. Not a vacation. A regular Tuesday in the life you want. What time do you wake up? Where are you? What does the morning look like? How do you spend 9 to 5? Who are you with? How does the evening end? Write it in enough detail that a stranger could film it.

Cost it out. What does that Tuesday actually cost per year? Housing, food, transportation, healthcare, discretionary. Be precise. Don't default to a number you've absorbed from culture. Price the life you described, not the life you think you should describe.

Calculate your freedom number. Annual cost divided by 0.04. That's the portfolio size that funds your Tuesday indefinitely at a 4% withdrawal rate. That's your enough.

Calculate your current gap. Distance from here to there. How long at your current savings rate? This is a compass bearing, not a judgment.

Answer one hard question: if you had your freedom number tomorrow and never needed to earn another dollar, what would you do with your time? If the answer comes easily, good. If it doesn't, that's the real work. Not the money. The meaning.

The money is a tool. This exercise makes sure you know what you're building with it. And if you're building toward a number you've never questioned, this is the chapter where you stop running long enough to check the map.

When Izzy said she needed "the right amount of the right work," she handed me a compass I didn't know I was missing. I hope this chapter does the same for you.

PART FOUR

The Think Again Loop: Recalibrate

CHAPTER 10

The Master Mind: Your Network Is Not Your Net Worth (But It Helps)

Hill's Principle: "The coordination of knowledge and effort between two or more people."

The worst career advice of the last 30 years is five words long: "Your network is your net worth."

It's not that the advice is entirely wrong. Relationships matter enormously for wealth-building. But the way that phrase has been interpreted, as a mandate to collect human beings like trading cards and to evaluate every social interaction through the lens of "what can this person do for me," has produced a generation of professionals who have 5,000 LinkedIn connections and zero people they can call at 2 AM when their business is falling apart.

I've been to networking events. You've been to networking events. We both know what they look like. A hotel ballroom. Bad coffee. A man who hands you his business card within 30 seconds of learning your name and then scans the room for someone more important while pretending to listen to your answer. That man has optimized for network size. He has not optimized for network value. And network value is not a function of how many people you know. It's a function of how many people trust you enough to be honest with you, challenge you, and combine their intelligence with yours in pursuit of a shared goal.

That's what Hill meant by the Master Mind, and his concept has been almost completely buried under three decades of networking culture that replaced depth with volume.

* * *

Hill defined the Master Mind as the coordination of knowledge and effort, in a spirit of harmony, between two or more people for a definite purpose. The critical phrases are "spirit of harmony" and "definite purpose." This is not a Meetup. Not a Slack channel with 300 members. Not a LinkedIn group. This is a small, committed, trust-based alliance of people who are working toward compatible goals and are willing to share knowledge, resources, and honest feedback.

Hill believed this alliance created a "third mind," a group intelligence exceeding the sum of its parts. He attributed it to metaphysics. The real explanation is cognitive diversity and distributed intelligence. When three or four people with different skill sets, different blind spots, and different networks focus on a shared problem, each person sees dimensions the others miss. The group produces solutions no individual member would have reached alone. It's not mystical. It's mathematics. More perspectives means more dimensions of a problem illuminated simultaneously.

I've been in three Master Mind groups over the last decade. The first was terrible: five people from the same industry with the same perspective, meeting monthly to confirm each other's existing beliefs. Echo chamber, not Master Mind. The second was better: four people from different fields, but we met too infrequently and accountability eroded. The third is the one that works, and it works because we learned from the failures of the first two.

What makes the third one work: four people, four different industries, biweekly video calls, 90 minutes each. We open with wins. We move to challenges. We close with commitments. And we follow up. When someone says "I'm going to close two new clients by the 15th," we ask on the 16th: "Did you?" Not with judgment. With genuine investment in each other's outcomes.

That group has been worth more to my professional and financial life than any course, conference, or book I've consumed. Not because the members are geniuses (though they're sharp). Because the structure creates accountability, the diversity creates insight, and the trust creates a space where you can say "I'm stuck" without performing competence.

* * *

Mark Granovetter published a paper in 1973 that reshaped how sociologists understand the value of relationships. His finding was counterintuitive: the most valuable connections for career advancement and opportunity discovery aren't your closest friends. They're your acquaintances.

Your strong ties (close friends, family, inner circle) tend to know the same people you know and access the same information. They live in your world. Your weak ties (the former colleague you email twice a year, the person you chatted with at a conference, your spouse's coworker you met at a barbecue) move in different circles, access different information, and see different opportunities.

Granovetter found that people who found jobs through personal contacts overwhelmingly found them through weak ties. Not because strong ties don't care. Because strong ties don't have new information to share.

The financial implication: your next opportunity is almost certainly going to come from someone you kind of know, not someone you know well. Which means maintaining a broad network of loose but genuine connections isn't vanity. It's opportunity surface area.

The sweet spot is both: a small Master Mind for depth (three to five people who challenge you, hold you accountable, and tell you the truth) and a broader network of weak ties for breadth (people across different industries who you stay in genuine but low-frequency contact with). Depth for wisdom. Breadth for opportunity.

* * *

Adam Grant's research on reciprocity styles adds a crucial filter. Grant categorizes people as givers (contribute more than they take), takers (extract more than they contribute), or matchers (aim for reciprocity).

His data reveals that givers occupy both the top and the bottom of the success distribution. The bottom-dwelling givers give indiscriminately, let takers exploit them, and burn out.

The top-performing givers give generously but strategically: they invest in other givers and matchers, set boundaries, and protect themselves from takers.

Your Master Mind should be 100% givers and matchers. This is a non-negotiable filter. One taker in a Master Mind group will poison the trust, monopolize the airtime, and extract value without contributing. I've seen it happen. The taker doesn't even realize they're doing it, which makes it harder to address and more important to prevent.

How to identify takers: watch how they treat people who can't do anything for them. Notice whether they follow up only when they need something. Observe whether they celebrate your wins or redirect every conversation back to themselves. Pay attention to whether they reciprocate your generosity or simply accept it as their due. The data reveals itself within two or three interactions if you're paying attention.

* * *

Robert Putnam documented the decline of social capital in America in Bowling Alone, and the trends he identified in 2000 have accelerated dramatically. Remote work eliminated the office as a social connector. Social media replaced community with performative connection.

And the result is that millions of people, particularly men between 25 and 45, have fewer close relationships than any generation in recorded history.

This matters for wealth-building because social capital is economic capital. Trust is currency. Every significant financial opportunity I've had, every partnership, every referral, every collaboration, came through a relationship. Not a resume. Not an application. A relationship.

The Master Mind isn't just a wealth strategy. In an era of epidemic disconnection, it's infrastructure for a functional life. The financial benefits are real. The psychological benefits, having people who know your real situation, who challenge your assumptions, who notice when you're drifting, might be worth even more.

I want to name something directly, because the market for AI "accountability partners" and "AI mastermind" tools is growing and the pitch is compelling: always available, never judgmental, infinitely patient, available at 2 AM. (Available at 2 AM, frankly, is sometimes the problem.)

It isn't a Master Mind.

A Master Mind requires mutual vulnerability. The willingness to share your actual numbers, your real fears, your honest struggles with people who have skin in the game alongside yours. An AI has none of those stakes. It cannot call you out with the authority of someone who shared last quarter's failure with you.

It cannot notice you've been quieter than usual for three meetings and ask what's wrong. It cannot be hurt by your not showing up. Trust, the load-bearing element of everything Hill described, requires relational stakes that no tool can manufacture. The AI is rooting for you the same way a vending machine is rooting for you. Politely. Indifferently. Without consequence.

The AI accountability app is useful. It is not this.

* * *

Let me get operational, because Hill described the Master Mind concept beautifully and gave approximately zero actionable instructions for building one.

Size:

Three to five people. Larger groups lose intimacy and accountability. Every additional person dilutes the trust.

Composition:

Cognitive diversity is mandatory. Different industries, different skill sets, different life experiences. The person who challenges your assumptions is more valuable than the person who confirms them. If everyone agrees with you all the time, you've built a support group, not a Master Mind.

Cadence:

Biweekly. Weekly feels like a job. Monthly loses momentum. Ninety minutes per meeting. Open with wins (builds positive reinforcement). Move to challenges (where the real value lives). Close with commitments (creates accountability for the next meeting).

Trust:

Non-negotiable foundation. If you can't share your real numbers, your real fears, and your honest struggles, the group is theater. Trust requires vulnerability, which requires time, which requires consistency. Don't expect deep trust by meeting two. Expect it by meeting five or six if everyone is showing up honestly.

Accountability:

Commitments must be tracked. "I'm going to reach out to five prospects" isn't a commitment without a follow-up. The group asks, with support, not judgment: "You said you'd do X. Did you? What happened? How can we help?"

* * *

What a Good Meeting Sounds Like

Let me give you a specific example of a Master Mind meeting that produced real financial value, so this concept feels less abstract.

About a year ago, I brought a pricing problem to my group. I'd been undercharging for a consulting service, knew it intellectually, but couldn't bring myself to raise the rate. The Big Snooze was in full effect. I'd anchored to my original price, and every time I considered increasing it, my brain generated catastrophic scenarios: clients will leave, they'll think I'm greedy, who am I to charge that much.

The group did what a good Master Mind does: they asked uncomfortable questions. One member, who runs a completely different type of business, asked how many clients I'd lost to price sensitivity in the last year. The answer was zero. Another asked what the client would pay if they had to replace me. I didn't know, but the question forced me to research it. The market rate was 35% higher than what I was charging.

A third member, the one who always pushes hardest, said something I think about constantly: "You're not doing your clients a favor by undercharging. You're training them to undervalue the work. And you're training yourself to believe it's worth less than it is."

I raised my rate by 25% the following month. Not one client left. Two said they'd expected the increase sooner. The annual impact on my income was significant. And none of it would have happened without four people in a video call asking me questions I was too close to the problem to ask myself.

That's the Master Mind. Not a networking event. Not a LinkedIn group. Four people who trust each other enough to say the uncomfortable thing, and who have enough cognitive diversity to see the angles you can't.

* * *

The Inner Circle Audit: This Week's Challenge

Map your current relational infrastructure. It takes 20 minutes and might reveal that you've been trying to build wealth in relational isolation without realizing it.

List the five people you spend the most professional or entrepreneurial time with. These might be colleagues, peers, mentors, or friends you talk to about money, career, and ambition.

For each, answer honestly: Do they challenge me or just agree with me? Do their skills and perspectives complement mine or duplicate them? Do they follow through on their own commitments? Are they givers, matchers, or takers?

Identify the gap. What perspective, skill set, or type of challenge is missing from your circle? Maybe you have plenty of creative thinkers but nobody with financial expertise. Maybe everyone is in your industry. Maybe nobody pushes back on your ideas.

List three specific people, existing contacts or reachable acquaintances, who could fill that gap. Real, accessible humans. Not fantasy mentors.

Reach out to one of them this week. The message doesn't need to be elaborate: "I'm building a small group of people who meet regularly to support each other's professional growth. I think you'd add a perspective we're missing. Would you be interested in a conversation about it?"

That's it. One honest invitation. The Master Mind doesn't assemble itself. It starts with one person deciding that they're done trying to build alone.

CHAPTER 11

Energy Management: Let's Talk About What

Hill Actually Meant (Sort Of)

Hill's Principle: "The transmutation of sex energy into creative achievement."

We need to talk about the chapter title.

Not my chapter title. Hill's. He called it "sex transmutation," and I want to acknowledge this openly because pretending it doesn't exist would be dishonest, and explaining it without wincing would be impossible.

Hill argued that highly successful people channel their sexual drive into productive endeavors. He believed this redirected energy was the source of genius, charisma, and creative magnetism. And buried under the layer of language that sounds like it belongs in a very specific corner of the internet is a legitimate insight about human energy management that deserves to be rescued from its own framing.

What Hill was actually describing, stripped of the Victorian discomfort, is this: human beings have a finite supply of creative, emotional, and physical energy. The way you allocate that energy determines the quality and quantity of everything you produce. People who protect their energy, who direct it deliberately instead of letting it leak in every direction, produce more meaningful work than people who don't.

That's a genuinely important idea. So let's keep the engine and drop the name that makes everyone uncomfortable at dinner parties.

* * *

Mihaly Csikszentmihalyi (I've practiced pronouncing it and I'm still only about 70% there) spent decades studying flow: a state of complete absorption where time distorts, self-consciousness disappears, and performance peaks. His research showed that people are happiest, most productive, and most creative inside this state.

Flow isn't accidental. It has preconditions: the task must be challenging enough to require full attention but not so overwhelming that it paralyzes. You need clear goals and immediate feedback. And critically, you need freedom from interruption. Flow is fragile. A single notification can shatter it, and re-entry takes 15 to 25 minutes.

This is the mechanism Hill was groping toward. Flow is what happens when you direct all available cognitive energy toward a single productive task. Nothing leaking to social media. Nothing bleeding into email anxiety. Nothing dissipating into the fake productivity of multitasking, which research has definitively shown doesn't exist. What we call multitasking is rapid task-switching, and it degrades performance on everything involved.

I track my flow states informally. On a good day, I achieve two to three blocks of genuine flow, totaling about four hours. Those four hours produce more valuable output than the other six hours of my workday combined. Not because I'm slacking for six hours. Because fragmented attention produces fragmented results, and focused attention produces concentrated value.

The financial implication: an hour of flow is worth approximately three hours of distracted work. If you can restructure your day to protect flow conditions, you functionally multiply your productive capacity without working more hours. That's not a productivity hack. That's an economic advantage.

* * *

Matthew Walker's sleep research should alarm anyone who treats sleep deprivation as a badge of productivity honor.

Less than seven hours of sleep and your prefrontal cortex, the brain region responsible for executive function, decision-making, creativity, and emotional regulation, goes partially offline. Your amygdala, which handles emotional reactivity, goes into overdrive. Your ability to consolidate memories, which is how learning becomes permanent, drops by up to 40%.

In plain language: when you don't sleep, you make worse decisions, have fewer creative insights, react more emotionally, and retain less of what you learn. You become a cognitively diminished version of yourself and then try to make financial decisions from that diminished state.

The wealth culture that celebrates "I'll sleep when I'm dead" and "grind while they sleep" is prescribing cognitive self-sabotage as a virtue. The person sleeping five hours and working 18 is not outproducing the person sleeping eight and working 10 with full cognitive function. They're working more hours at a fraction of their capacity and calling it discipline.

I tested this in my own life after reading Walker's research. I tracked my output quality (not just quantity) across a month, cross-referencing with sleep data from a fitness tracker. The correlation was embarrassingly clear. On nights with seven-plus hours, my next-day output was sharper, more creative, and required fewer revisions. On nights with less than six hours, I produced more words but worse words, and the revision time more than consumed whatever extra hours I'd "gained" by sleeping less.

Sleep is not the opposite of productivity. Sleep is when your brain consolidates learning, processes emotions, repairs neural infrastructure, and prepares for the next day of high-level thinking. Cutting it isn't gaining time. It's borrowing against cognitive capacity at a brutal interest rate.

* * *

Your energy runs on cycles that the industrial work model ignores entirely.

Nathaniel Kleitman identified what he called the basic rest-activity cycle: approximately 90-minute alternations of higher and lower alertness throughout the day. For roughly 90 minutes, your cognitive function is elevated. Then, for about 20 minutes, your brain needs recovery. Then the cycle repeats.

Elite performers across domains, from concert pianists to surgeons to Olympic athletes, intuitively structure their work around these cycles. They practice intensely for 60 to 90 minutes, then rest genuinely. They don't attempt to sustain peak performance for eight hours straight because it's physiologically impossible.

The application: structure deep work in 90-minute blocks followed by real 15-to-20-minute recovery. Not "recovery" where you check email on your phone. Actual recovery. Walk. Stretch. Stare at a wall. Let your brain do nothing. The nothing is when your cognitive battery recharges. Skip it and you'll run each subsequent block on declining voltage.

Three 90-minute blocks per day equals 4.5 hours of genuine deep work. That will outproduce most people's 10-hour days because their 10 hours are filled with interruptions, context-switching, performative busyness, and "quick" social media checks that each cost 23 minutes of re-engagement.

AI tools introduce a new wrinkle here worth naming. Used well, meaning research batching, first-draft generation, analysis during a focused work block, AI amplifies the output of your deep work window without fragmenting it. Used carelessly, AI assistants add to the notification load: alerts, suggestions, model responses demanding immediate engagement. Same predator. New camouflage.

The energy principle is the same one Kleitman identified: protect the 90-minute block from anything that demands a context switch. Whether the interruption comes from email, Slack, or an AI assistant that just finished your task is irrelevant. The cost to re-engagement is the same 23 minutes either way.

* * *

Exercise is the energy investment with the highest documented cognitive return, and almost nobody frames it as a financial strategy.

John Ratey at Harvard synthesized decades of research in Spark: regular cardiovascular exercise increases BDNF (brain-derived neurotrophic factor), promoting new neural connections. It improves executive function, working memory, emotional regulation, and creativity. It reduces anxiety and depression more effectively than many pharmaceutical interventions.

Exercise literally makes you smarter, more creative, more emotionally stable, and more resilient. Not metaphorically. Measurably.

Yet most ambitious people treat it as the first thing to cut when they get busy. That's like refusing to sharpen the axe because you're too busy chopping trees.

Thirty minutes of cardiovascular exercise, three to five times per week, is a cognitive performance enhancer. Over a career, the cumulative advantage of a person who exercises regularly versus one who doesn't is probably worth more in lifetime earnings than most professional development investments. I can't prove that with a controlled study. But I can tell you that every high-performing person I know personally, every single one, has a consistent exercise habit. That's not coincidence. That's signal.

* * *

The final energy drain Hill couldn't have anticipated: chronic digital overstimulation.

Anna Lembke at Stanford has documented how constant digital stimulation downregulates dopamine receptors, creating a state where the very activities that build wealth, the ones requiring sustained effort and delayed gratification, feel neurologically unrewarding compared to the effortless hits from a phone. You don't just lose time to the scroll. You lose the neurological capacity for hard, meaningful work. The dopamine baseline drops, the effort threshold rises, and the phone isn't just stealing hours. It's stealing the cognitive fuel those hours run on.

The full mechanism, and what to do about it over seven deliberately structured days, is in Chapter 12. For the purpose of this chapter: your screen diet is your energy diet. It belongs in your Energy Audit data. Track it this week and let the numbers tell you what your gut has been suspecting.

* * *

The Correlation I Didn't Want to See

I mentioned tracking my energy levels against output quality earlier. Let me share the finding that was most uncomfortable, because uncomfortable findings are usually the valuable ones.

Over a three-month tracking period, I found a near-perfect correlation between my phone screen time and the quality of my financial decision-making. On days when screen time exceeded three hours, I was significantly more likely to make impulsive purchases, skip my deep work block, and delay financial tasks I'd committed to. On days when screen time was under 90 minutes, my follow-through rate on financial commitments was above 85%.

The correlation wasn't causal in the scientific sense. I didn't run a controlled experiment. But the pattern was consistent enough over 90 days that I stopped treating it as coincidence and started treating it as signal.

Here's what I think is happening: high screen time depletes the same cognitive resources needed for financial discipline. Decision fatigue from constant micro-choices (what to click, what to watch, what to scroll past) leaves nothing in the tank for the macro-choices (should I invest, should I negotiate, should I stick to the budget). The phone isn't just stealing time. It's stealing the cognitive capacity for financial self-control.

This finding changed my daily architecture. My phone now stays in another room until after my first deep work block. Financial decision-making happens in the morning, when cognitive resources are fresh. Impulse-purchase temptations get routed through the 72-hour implementation intention. The structure isn't willpower. It's engineering, designed around a data pattern I can't un-see.

The neurological reason this correlation exists, why screen time depletes the precise cognitive resources that financial discipline requires, is in Chapter 12, along with the seven-day protocol for resetting it.

* * *

The Energy Audit: This Week's Challenge

Seven days of data collection. It's tedious. The data is worth it.

Three times daily (morning, midday, evening), rate your energy on a 1-to-10 scale. Also log: hours of sleep the night before, whether you exercised, total screen time (your phone tracks this), and what your primary work activity was during each rating period.

At the end of the week, look for three patterns. When is your energy highest? That window should contain your most important deep work, not email and meetings. How does sleep correlate with next-day energy? How does screen time correlate with focus quality?

Most people discover three things, and all three are uncomfortable. First, they're sleeping less than they think. Second, their highest-energy window is being wasted on low-value tasks. Third, their phone is consuming two to four hours daily that they genuinely didn't realize they were spending.

Based on the data, make three changes. Protect your highest-energy window for deep work. Add one 30-minute exercise session to your lowest-energy day. Implement a specific daily screen time limit and track compliance for the remaining six days.

Hill wanted you to channel your energy toward achievement. The upgrade: measure where your energy actually goes, stop the leaks, protect the peaks, and build the biological foundation (sleep, exercise, cognitive recovery) that makes everything else in this book possible. Without this chapter, every other principle runs on a depleted battery. With it, every principle runs at full voltage.

CHAPTER 12

The Mind-Brain Advantage:

Cognitive Sovereignty in the Age of Distraction

Hill's Principles: "The subconscious mind is the connecting link between the finite mind of man and Infinite Intelligence." And: "The brain is a broadcasting and receiving station for thought."

It is 11:47 PM. The phone is six inches from your face. You are scrolling through a thread about interest rate predictions, or unrest in some country you couldn't locate on a map last week, or someone's opinion about someone else's opinion about a stock you do not own. You are not learning anything. You read the same analysis from three different sources earlier today. You are just feeding a compulsion, pouring stimulation into a brain that does not need more information but cannot stop seeking it.

If any of that sounds familiar, stay with me, because somewhere inside that scroll there is a moment of genuine out-of-body clarity available to you: *this device is remodeling my brain right now.* Not metaphorically. Physically. The neural pathways for compulsive checking, for short-burst stimulation, for novelty-seeking without purpose, are getting stronger with every swipe. And the pathways for sustained focus, for deep creative work, for the kind of patient thinking that actually builds wealth, are weakening from disuse.

This is the chapter where we put the phone down. In another room. And we lie in the dark for about ten minutes feeling genuinely unsettled, because the thing we have been treating as a harmless habit is, at the neurological level, actively sabotaging the cognitive infrastructure we need to do everything else in this book. Welcome to the part where the cost shows up on the balance sheet.

Napoleon Hill gave us two principles for this territory. The first said the subconscious mind is the link between human intelligence and something he called Infinite Intelligence. The second said the brain is a broadcasting and receiving station for thought, sending and receiving on frequencies of concentrated desire. Strip away the metaphysics from both, and what remains is something that neuroscience has now validated beyond reasonable dispute: your brain physically restructures itself based on what you repeatedly feed it. That restructuring determines what you notice, what you pursue, what you believe is possible, and what you actually build.

The upgrade: Hill was right about the mechanism. He was wrong about the frequency band. Your thoughts don't broadcast into the cosmos. They broadcast into your own neural architecture. And that is, if anything, more consequential than the cosmic version he imagined.

The Clay That Never Hardens

Neuroplasticity, the brain's ability to reorganize itself by forming new neural connections throughout life, is one of the most consequential discoveries in the history of neuroscience. Norman Doidge documented cases that would sound like science fiction if they weren't backed by imaging data: stroke patients retraining undamaged brain regions to assume destroyed functions, elderly adults growing new neural pathways by learning instruments late in life. The brain isn't fixed hardware after some critical developmental window. It is clay that never stops being moldable. Which means you, sitting wherever you're sitting, with whatever financial story you've been telling yourself for whatever number of years, are still being shaped right now. By something. The only question is by what.

The operating principle: neurons that fire together wire together. Repeat a thought pattern, practice a behavior, inhabit a mental state, and the neural pathway for that pattern grows faster, stronger, and more automatic. This is how habits form, how skills develop, and how financial beliefs embed so deeply they feel like personality rather than programming.

This is simultaneously the best and the worst news about your financial life.

The best news: your beliefs about money are not permanent. The neural pathways telling you "I'm bad with money" or "people like me don't build wealth" were constructed by repeated experience and reinforcement. They can be deconstructed and rebuilt through different repeated experience. The entire book you are holding has been leveraging this principle, whether I named it or not.

The worst news: your environment is remodeling your brain whether you consent or not. Every hour of passive scrolling strengthens pathways for distraction and short-burst reward. Every anxious news cycle deepens the grooves of scarcity thinking. Your brain doesn't evaluate whether these pathways serve your goals. It just builds more infrastructure for whatever you practice most. The brain is a yes-and improv partner. It will take whatever you give it and run with it. So give it something good.

Which brings us to the part of the chapter that actually hurts.

The Enemy Within

A few years back, a client of mine, Diane Walsh, bought a piece of equipment for a business venture. It cost $4,200. She knew it was overpriced. She'd found comparable options for $2,800. She bought the $4,200 version anyway, because the first listing she'd encountered, before she'd done any research, was $5,900. By the time she found the "discounted" $4,200 option, her brain wasn't comparing it to the market. It was comparing it to $5,900. And $4,200 next to $5,900 felt like a steal.

She was anchored. The first number she saw had set an invisible reference point, and every subsequent evaluation ran through it. She overpaid by at least $1,000 because of a listing she had immediately dismissed as irrelevant. The listing she dismissed was, mechanically, the one driving the decision.

That's one bias. There are over 180 documented, and they don't operate in isolation. Pleasant.

Daniel Kahneman spent his career demonstrating that human beings are systematically (not occasionally) irrational about money. His framework divides cognition into two systems. System 1 is fast and automatic, running on pattern recognition and emotion, and operates below conscious awareness roughly 95% of the time. System 2 is slow and deliberate, and does the actual analytical work. The uncomfortable truth: you think you're in System 2 most of the time. You're not. System 1 is driving. System 2 is in the passenger seat, reading a magazine, reasonably confident it's in charge.

System 1 is riddled with exploitable patterns. Five of the most financially expensive:

Confirmation bias. You seek information confirming what you already believe and filter out contradictions. When Diane was enthusiastic about that overpriced equipment, she read three positive reviews and skimmed the critical ones. The critical reviews had the information she actually needed. Her brain had already made the emotional decision and was now running a search for justification. The brain is an excellent attorney for whatever side hired it first.

Anchoring bias. Already demonstrated. In salary negotiations, whoever names a number first owns the room. If you open at $85,000 when the market rate is $110,000, you may never close that gap, not because you can't negotiate, but because the anchor holds.

Loss aversion. Losing $100 feels about twice as painful as gaining $100 feels good. This asymmetry produces a specific financial pathology: holding losing investments too long (selling makes the loss "real"), selling winners too early (locking in gains before they "disappear"), and declining reasonable opportunities because potential downside looms larger than equivalent upside. Tom Reilly, a friend in finance, held a bad investment for 14 months past the point where the data said exit, because selling meant admitting he was wrong. The loss tripled in those 14 months. Tom now talks about it like a recovering anything.

The availability heuristic. You estimate probability based on how easily you can recall an example. Because market crashes are vivid and memorable, investors overestimate the risk of total loss. Because successful founders are featured constantly in media, aspiring entrepreneurs overestimate their odds. Your perception of risk is not a calculation. It's a highlight reel curated by an algorithm that profits from your attention.

Status quo bias. You prefer things as they are because they are as they are. Switching banks, renegotiating insurance, updating your financial plan, all potentially beneficial, all resisted because the current state has the advantage of being current. A client of mine stayed with a bank charging monthly maintenance fees for two years because switching felt inconvenient. The inconvenience would have taken 45 minutes. The fees cost $288. Forty-five minutes for $288 is a pretty good hourly rate, but inertia, as always, was free.

Your brain is lying to you right now. Quietly. In ways that feel entirely rational. And every lie has a price tag attached.

The Counter-Arsenal

The answer is not to fix your biases. You can't. They're structural features of human cognition, not bugs that a patch will resolve. The answer is to build a latticework of corrective tools that catch your thinking before the biases finish running the numbers.

Charlie Munger spent his career assembling exactly this kind of latticework, mental models from multiple disciplines that check each other's blind spots. The insight behind the approach: most people think with the tools of their own profession and end up seeing every problem as the kind of nail their particular hammer was designed for. A broader set of tools produces genuinely better decisions. Or, less elegantly: don't bring a finance brain to a marriage problem.

Five models that have measurably saved real money for the clients I've coached, and frankly for me:

Inversion. Instead of asking "how do I succeed?" ask "how would I guarantee failure?" List everything that would definitely destroy the plan. Then design around those things. My own current financial system was built backward from a failure list: ignoring cash flow, making emotional investment decisions, letting lifestyle inflate with every income increase. The failures were clearer than the successes, and designing against them produced a more robust system than any success-focused planning session I've run.

Second-order thinking. Consider what happens after the first consequence. Cutting prices increases sales volume (first order). It also trains customers to expect discounts, compresses margins, and selects for price-sensitive buyers who will leave the moment a competitor goes lower (second order). Most financial decisions that look brilliant at the first-order level become disasters at the second. The smart move at move one is often the dumb position at move four.

Circle of competence. Only operate in domains you genuinely understand. The most expensive financial mistakes I've seen, in my own life and in the people I coach, came from acting outside competence with the confidence of someone who thought they were inside it. The pattern is remarkably consistent. People rarely lose money in areas where they deeply understand the mechanics. Significant losses tend to occur where knowledge is thinner than confidence.

Margin of safety. Engineers build bridges to handle twice the expected load. Financial plans deserve equivalent engineering. Six months of emergency savings, not two. Revenue projections at 70% of optimistic estimates. Timelines at 150% of original plans. The world is uncertain, and your forecasts are wrong more often than your conviction suggests. Plan for the version of reality where things are 30% worse than you imagined, and you'll spend most of your life pleasantly surprised.

Map versus territory. Your financial model is not your financial reality. Your spreadsheet is not your business. Hold models lightly, update them frequently, and never fall in love with the elegance of a projection at the expense of paying attention to the messy, contradictory data the real world keeps offering. The map is also not the meal. Stop eating the menu.

The Thermostat's Coalition

T. Harv Eker introduced the concept of the financial thermostat: a subconscious wealth set-point your brain defends, generating self-sabotaging behavior whenever your actual financial position deviates too far from the set-point in either direction.

What Eker's framework doesn't fully explain is *why* the thermostat is so hard to move. After the preceding chapters of this book, the answer is visible: the thermostat isn't one thing. It's a coalition. And coalitions are harder to dismantle than individuals, ask any government.

Status quo bias keeps you at the set-point by making change feel inherently risky. Confirmation bias filters your incoming information to reinforce the set-point, serving you evidence that your current level is appropriate and natural. Loss aversion makes any upward deviation feel precarious: the higher you climb, the more you have to lose. Anchoring keeps you evaluating new opportunities relative to your current baseline rather than their absolute merit. Working together, these biases form a coordinated defense system that your brain has been constructing for decades.

This is why financial self-help books often produce temporary enthusiasm and permanent stagnation. Reading the book moves the conscious needle. The coalition holds the thermostat in place.

The mental models in the previous section are your counter-coalition. Inversion asks what behavior would guarantee staying at the current set-point. Second-order thinking reveals the downstream costs of staying exactly where you are. Circle of competence helps distinguish areas where the thermostat is calibrated by genuine experience versus areas where it's calibrated by fear. Neuroplasticity is the mechanism that, over time, actually moves the dial, by physically rewiring the pathways the coalition runs on.

Awareness doesn't dissolve the coalition. But awareness plus deliberate systems, the combination this entire book has been building, erodes it. Not overnight. In iterations. Each loop of the Think Again cycle moves the set-point a fraction further in the direction you've chosen. Compound interest, but for who you are.

The Filter You Didn't Know You Had

Your brain has a structure called the reticular activating system, or RAS, that explains something Hill attributed to cosmic attraction.

At any given moment, your senses process approximately 11 million bits of information per second. Your conscious mind handles roughly 50. The RAS decides which 50 get through, selecting for relevance, novelty, and emotional significance based on instructions your goals and beliefs provide.

This is why, the moment you decide to buy a particular car, you suddenly see that car everywhere. The cars were always there. Your RAS wasn't flagging them before because they weren't defined as relevant. The same mechanism applies to financial opportunities, business ideas, and useful connections. When you define a specific financial goal with genuine clarity and emotional weight, your RAS begins filtering the world for information related to that goal. You notice the conversation at the next table that's directly relevant. You overhear an opportunity that would have sailed past you a month ago.

This isn't the universe responding to vibrations. It's your perceptual filter responding to instructions you gave it. Hill was right that focused thought changes what you perceive. He was right that the mechanism operates below conscious awareness. He just had the address wrong: it's in your brainstem, not the cosmos.

The Algorithm and Your Financial Brain

Here is what Hill couldn't have anticipated, and what makes this chapter's principles more urgent in 2026 than they were in 1937.

The cognitive biases you just read about, confirmation bias, anchoring, loss aversion, the availability heuristic, status quo bias, are no longer purely internal. They have been reverse-engineered, productized, and deployed against you at scale.

Every major platform you use runs on a recommendation system trained on your behavioral data. Every click, every pause, every scroll that slows down, all of it goes into a model whose job is to learn what keeps you engaged and serve you more of it. Confirmation bias isn't just a personal cognitive error anymore. It's an engineered product feature. The platform profits when you stay. You stay longest when you see content that confirms what you already believe. So the algorithm feeds you confirmation, at a speed and volume your unassisted brain could never generate on its own. It is a hall of mirrors, and the mirrors are paid by the click.

The thermostat and the algorithm form a feedback loop that is genuinely difficult to break. If your set-point is scarcity, you engage with scarcity-confirming content: housing crisis coverage, wage stagnation data, financial stress narratives. The algorithm notices. It serves more. Your RAS, trained on the new input diet, starts flagging threats and obstacles rather than opportunities. The set-point hardens. The coalition strengthens. And none of this is visible unless you know to look for it.

Anna Lembke's clinical research gives this the most alarming framing. Chronic overstimulation doesn't just steal attention. It alters dopamine baseline levels. When the reward system is constantly flooded with low-effort stimulation, the receptors downregulate. The result: activities requiring sustained effort feel less rewarding than they once did. The effort threshold for productive work rises. Building wealth, which depends on extended patience and tolerance of delayed gratification, becomes neurologically harder, not because you've gotten lazy, but because your brain's reward calibration has shifted toward the easier inputs it keeps receiving. "You're not lazy" is, by the way, the rare sentence in a wealth book that is actually true.

Lembke's prescription is a sustained reduction of high-stimulation inputs, what she calls a dopamine fast, to allow the system to recalibrate. The initial discomfort passes within days. What comes back on the other side is a recalibrated baseline where deep work feels engaging again, boredom becomes tolerable, and the sustained attention that every principle in this book requires becomes neurologically accessible rather than neurologically punishing. Naomi Brooks, a client who has run a quarterly version of this for two years, reports the same pattern Lembke's clinical work documents: each reset leaves a residue. Slightly less compulsion. Slightly more stillness. Slightly easier access to flow. After a year of quarterly resets, her default screen time dropped roughly 35% even during the non-fast weeks. The plasticity works in both directions. You can rebuild toward focus as deliberately as the algorithms built toward distraction.

There are also three constructive applications of AI worth naming directly. First: AI tools can function as a legitimate Pre-Mortem partner (Chapter 6) and as a Socratic interlocutor for surfacing inherited financial beliefs. Ask an AI to argue against your investment thesis with no emotional investment in being polite, and it will identify weaknesses your confirmation bias has suppressed. Second: the same neuroplasticity principle applies to AI-assisted cognitive reframing exercises, where AI helps you generate evidence-based alternative interpretations of financial setbacks and write new money narratives in real time. Third, and most practically: if your AI content feed is consistently serving you anxiety, comparison, and scarcity, that is data about what your RAS has been trained to flag. Changing the input deliberately changes the filter. Yes, the same machine that helped break your attention can help you reassemble it. That is not irony. That is leverage.

The solution to the algorithmic threat is not outrage. It is the same environmental engineering that every chapter in this book has been building: redesign the input conditions, because your brain becomes what it is repeatedly fed.

Which is, in fact, what James Allen understood in 1903, before any of us had heard of a neural pathway.

The Garden

Allen wrote *As a Man Thinketh* over a century before anyone had heard of neuroplasticity. His central metaphor: the mind is a garden. Thoughts are seeds. What you cultivate determines what grows. Neglect the garden and weeds take over. Tend it deliberately and you harvest what you planted.

It is a metaphor, not science. But it maps onto the neuroscience with uncanny precision. Your neural pathways are the garden. Repeated thoughts and behaviors are the seeds. Neuroplasticity is the soil. And the modern digital environment, with its engineered stimulation, its algorithmically amplified biases, and its relentless installation of financial anxiety, is the equivalent of someone dumping invasive weed seeds over your fence every night while you sleep. And selling you the herbicide in the morning.

Allen couldn't have known that brain imaging would literally validate his metaphor 120 years later. He sensed it. Hill sensed it. Every wisdom tradition that ever said "guard your thoughts" was pointing at the same phenomenon Norman Doidge's research confirmed: what you repeatedly feed your brain, it builds more architecture for.

The practical difference between Allen's era and ours is the scale of the threat. Allen's garden had to contend with a limited number of weeds: gossip, newspapers, the occasional toxic relationship. Your garden is under sustained assault from a globally networked, algorithmically optimized, behaviorally engineered weed-delivery system that operates 24 hours a day and fits in your pocket. Allen had it easy.

The work of this chapter isn't passive. It requires active, deliberate cultivation. You know your dominant biases now: plant corrective models against them. You know your thermostat's coalition:

build the counter-coalition, one habit and one decision journal entry at a time. You know what your RAS is filtering for: feed it better instructions. And you know who has been holding the chisel while you weren't paying attention.

Take it back.

This Week's Challenge: Two-Part Mind-Brain Audit

Twenty-five minutes total. Do both parts in the same sitting.

Part A: The Bias Audit (15 minutes)

Think about your last three significant financial decisions. Investments, major purchases, career moves, business commitments. Anything involving meaningful money or time.

For each decision, identify which biases were most likely operating. Were you anchored to the first number you encountered? Were you seeking confirmation?

Were you avoiding a loss rather than pursuing a gain? Were you overestimating a risk because a bad outcome was vivid in your memory? Were you staying with the status quo because change felt like work?

Be ruthless. The point is not self-punishment. It is pattern recognition. You are looking for your default bias, the one that showed up across multiple decisions, the one your System 1 reaches for first.

For the decision you feel least confident about in retrospect, apply three mental models. Invert it:

what would have guaranteed failure? Think second-order: what downstream consequences did you miss or discount? Check the margin of safety: how much room for error did you actually leave?

Start a decision journal today. For every significant financial decision going forward, record: the decision itself, your reasoning in the moment, the expected outcome, which biases you suspect were active, and the date. Review it quarterly. Within a year, you will have a personal map of your cognitive blind spots that is worth more than any advisor's opinion, because it is built from your actual decision-making patterns rather than generic demographic assumptions.

Part B: The Digital Detox Protocol (7 days)

One honest measurement at each end. Four deliberate changes in between.

Day 1: Measure. Check your phone's screen time report. Write down total daily hours, your top three apps, and your daily pickups. This is your current neurological diet, printed in black and white. Most people are genuinely shocked by the number. Record it without judgment. You can't change what you haven't named.

Day 2: Add friction. Move your three highest-consumption non-essential apps into a folder on your phone's last screen. Do not delete them. Just make the habitual reach require one extra step. That single additional action is enough to interrupt the automatic behavior and create a moment of actual choice, which is all you need to stop acting like a system and start acting like a person.

Day 3: Install blackouts. No screens for the first 60 minutes after waking and the last 60 minutes before sleep. Replace the morning scroll with literally anything else: coffee on the porch, a few pages of something physical, silence, staring at the ceiling while your brain remembers what boredom feels like. Replace the evening scroll with anything analog.

Days 4 through 6: Protect deep work. One 90-minute block per day with your phone in another room (not on silent in your pocket, in another room) and your computer notifications off. Use this block for the single most important financial or professional task on your list. Notice how focus quality changes across the three days. That shift is neuroplasticity in real time.

Day 7: Measure again. Compare screen time and daily pickups to Day 1. More importantly, note how you feel. Is sustained focus easier than it was six days ago? Is boredom more tolerable? Are you sleeping better?

Most people report a 30 to 50 percent reduction in screen time and a noticeable improvement in both mood and cognitive sharpness. Some make the changes permanent. Some reset. Both are fine.

The point is to give your brain a direct experience of what uncompromised cognitive function feels like, so you can make an informed decision about what you want your neurological diet to look like going forward.

Hill said the subconscious mind shapes your reality, and the brain transmits and receives thought. He was right on both counts. The upgrade: your subconscious is shaped by systematic errors that can be named, cataloged, and partially corrected. Your brain transmits and receives based on whatever you have been repeatedly feeding it.

Your brain is still being sculpted every day.

The only question is whether you're holding the chisel, or someone else is.

CHAPTER 13

The Sixth Sense: Intuition, Pattern Recognition, and Trusting Your Gut (With Data)

Hill's Principle: "The sixth sense is the creative imagination's receiving set."

A few years ago, I was evaluating a business partnership that looked perfect on paper. The numbers worked. The skill sets were complementary. The market opportunity was clear. My spreadsheet said yes. My analysis said yes. Every rational input pointed toward proceeding.

And something in my gut said no.

I couldn't articulate it. There was no specific red flag, no smoking gun, no clear data point that justified the feeling. It was just a sensation, somewhere between my sternum and my stomach, that something was off. The kind of feeling you learn to notice only after you've ignored it enough times and paid the price.

I listened to my gut. I declined the partnership. And about eight months later, I learned through mutual contacts that the person I'd almost partnered with had a pattern of over-promising, under-delivering, and leaving collaborators holding financial obligations. My gut had picked up a signal my spreadsheet couldn't detect.

But here's the thing: I've also ignored my gut and been right to ignore it. I've had the same queasy feeling before investments that turned out to be excellent. I've had the same "something's off" sensation before business decisions that produced some of my best results. My gut isn't always right. It's a data source, not an oracle. And the challenge of Hill's sixth principle, modernized, is learning when that data source is reliable and when it's leading you off a cliff.

* * *

Gary Klein spent his career studying how experts make decisions in high-pressure environments. Firefighters who order evacuations seconds before a floor collapses. ICU nurses who detect patient deterioration before the monitors do. Chess grandmasters who see the winning move before they can explain why.

Klein's Recognition-Primed Decision model explains the mechanism: experts rarely weigh options analytically. They recognize patterns from vast experience, mentally simulate a course of action, and act. The entire process takes seconds. The conscious explanation comes later, if at all.

That firefighter who "just knew" the floor was about to give? When Klein reconstructed the unconscious logic, it turned out the fire was unusually quiet and the floor unusually hot, two cues that, cross-referenced against thousands of fires in the firefighter's experience, matched the pattern of a basement fire, meaning the floor was structurally compromised. His gut feeling was data processed too fast for conscious awareness to track.

The Getty Museum spent 14 months and significant money testing a supposedly ancient Greek statue with electron microscopy, X-ray diffraction, and mass spectrometry. Everything checked out. They bought it for millions. Then art historians took one look and felt something was wrong. They couldn't immediately explain why. They just knew. The statue was a forgery. Decades of expertise, compressed into a feeling, had detected what 14 months of scientific analysis had missed.

That's intuition. Not cosmic reception. Compressed experience.

* * *

The critical question is when to trust it, and Klein and Daniel Kahneman, who spent years on opposite sides of the intuition debate, published a joint paper in 2009 identifying the conditions that make gut feelings reliable.

Condition one: a regular environment with valid cues. The domain must have patterns that repeat consistently. An experienced nurse's intuition about patient deterioration is reliable because patient deterioration follows recognizable patterns. An investor's intuition about stock prices is unreliable because short-term price movements are largely random.

Condition two: extensive practice with feedback. You need thousands of repetitions with information about whether you were right or wrong. A negotiator who has closed 500 deals and tracked outcomes has calibrated intuition. An investor who only remembers their wins has biased intuition.

Condition three: low emotional arousal at the moment of decision. When you're calm, your intuition draws from your full experience base. When you're anxious, angry, or excited, it draws from emotionally charged memories, which may not be representative. The gut feeling you get during a market panic is almost certainly not your best data.

This framework now has a specific AI-era application that's worth making explicit.

In certain data-rich, patterned domains, AI pattern recognition is now demonstrably more reliable than human intuition. A model detecting portfolio rebalancing signals from market data has processed more historical cycles than any investor's gut could ever encode. An AI flagging fraud patterns in transaction data is catching signals too faint for conscious recognition. In these domains, the structured, data-dense ones with clear feedback loops, Klein and Kahneman's conditions for reliable intuition are met better by the model than by you. That is not an insult. It is a category. The model has processed more poker hands than you have eaten meals.

But flip the domain. Is this business partnership trustworthy? Is this opportunity real or a performance? Does this person's track record hold up under scrutiny? Your intuition, calibrated by years of reading people in this specific context, will almost always outperform an AI that has only the words on the screen to work with. The framework is unchanged. The question is simply: which kind of pattern is this?

My partnership decision met all three conditions. I'd evaluated dozens of potential collaborators over the years. I'd seen the outcomes of both good and bad partnerships. And I was calm when I made the assessment, not pressured or emotionally charged. My gut was drawing from a relevant, experienced, well-calibrated database.

But when I've felt queasy about a stock market investment during a downturn? That gut feeling was anchored to the emotional memory of losing money, not to a pattern-matched assessment of the investment's fundamentals. My gut was processing fear, not data.

* * *

Gerd Gigerenzer at the Max Planck Institute has shown something that further complicates the picture: in certain conditions, simple heuristics outperform sophisticated analysis. When predicting outcomes in uncertain environments with limited data, fast-and-frugal decision rules often beat complex models because each layer of analysis introduces another opportunity for cognitive bias to distort the result.

The simplest investing heuristic, buy a diversified index fund and don't touch it for decades, outperforms the vast majority of professional fund managers who use sophisticated models. Not because the analysis is wrong. Because the analysis is human, which means every analytical step is contaminated by overconfidence, loss aversion, anchoring, and the dozen other biases from the previous chapter.

Sometimes the smartest financial decision is the simplest one. Sometimes adding more analysis makes the outcome worse. The skill is knowing which situation you're in.

* * *

Your financial intuition is shaped by your financial history, and that history may not be a representative dataset.

If you grew up in a household where money was scarce, your gut is calibrated for scarcity: protect what you have, avoid risk, treat every expenditure as a threat. If you grew up in abundance, your gut might be calibrated for opportunity: spend freely, take risks, assume money regenerates.

Neither calibration is universally right. Both are patterns learned from a specific environment. And both can lead you catastrophically astray in a different environment. The scarcity-calibrated person might pass on a reasonable investment because their gut screams "danger" at any risk. The abundance-calibrated person might take reckless bets because their gut says "money always works out."

My own calibration skews toward scarcity. I grew up watching money be a source of stress, and my default gut response to financial risk is protective, conservative, sometimes irrationally so. Knowing this about myself has been one of the most valuable pieces of financial self-knowledge I've acquired, because it lets me apply a correction. When my gut says "too risky" and my analysis says "reasonable risk with adequate margin of safety," I know to weight the analysis more heavily because my gut is running outdated software from childhood.

* * *

I use a protocol I call the Gut-Check that reconciles intuition and analysis without surrendering to either.

Before any analysis, I check my gut and write down what it says. Not to act on it. To capture the signal before analysis drowns it out.

Then I do the analysis. Numbers, data, mental models, advisors.

Then I compare. If gut and analysis agree, I move forward with high confidence. If they disagree, I investigate the discrepancy. Can I trace the gut feeling to relevant experience in this specific domain? Or is it reacting to fear, childhood conditioning, or an emotionally charged memory? If I can trace it to experience, I weight it. If I can only trace it to emotion, I weight the analysis.

This protocol doesn't always produce the right answer. Nothing does. But it consistently produces better answers than either gut alone or analysis alone, because each one's strengths cover the other's blind spots.

* * *

When My Gut Was Wrong About Money

I told you about the partnership where my gut was right. Let me tell you about the investment where my gut was dead wrong, because calibration requires both data points.

In early 2020, the market dropped over 30% in a matter of weeks. My gut screamed to sell everything. The emotional memory of past losses lit up like a fire alarm. Every instinct said: get out, protect what you have, this is going to zero.

I almost listened. I had the sell orders drafted. My finger was on the button. Then I asked the three calibration questions: Am I experienced in this specific domain? (Moderate, not expert.) Is the environment patterned? (Long-term markets recover; short-term crashes are unpredictable.) Am I emotionally regulated right now? (Absolutely not. I was terrified.)

Two out of three conditions for reliable intuition were unmet. My gut wasn't processing pattern recognition. It was processing fear. I closed the sell orders. I didn't invest more (I wasn't confident enough for that). I just didn't sell.

Within 18 months, the market had recovered and exceeded previous highs. If I'd listened to my gut, I would have locked in a 30% loss and missed the recovery. The gut-check protocol, which was designed for exactly this kind of moment, saved me more money than any single investment decision I've ever made.

That experience permanently changed my relationship with financial intuition. I still listen to my gut. I just verify its credentials first.

* * *

The Gut-Check Journal: This Week's Challenge

Two weeks. Every financial decision, large or small. Build your personal accuracy database.

Before you analyze any financial decision, write your gut feeling in one sentence. "My gut says yes." "Something feels off." "This feels safe." Don't overthink it. Don't justify it. Just capture the first response.

Make the decision using your normal process.

Record the outcome when it becomes clear.

At the end of two weeks, calculate your gut accuracy rate. Where was your instinct right? Where was it wrong? Break it down by domain: are you more accurate about people than about numbers? About familiar situations than novel ones? About calm decisions than emotional ones?

Most people discover that their intuition is surprisingly reliable in domains where they have deep experience and surprisingly unreliable in domains where they're operating on emotion or thin knowledge. That pattern, once visible, becomes a permanent decision-making advantage. You know when to lean into your gut and when to override it with data. And that calibrated self-awareness, the knowledge of your own reliability map, is worth more than any single decision you'll ever make.

CHAPTER 14

The Modern Wealth Stack: Income, Equity, and Leverage in the 2020s

The chapter Hill never wrote because he was too busy talking about the ether.

Here is an uncomfortable truth that the financial content industry is built to obscure: the mechanics of building wealth are boring.

Earn more than you spend. Invest the difference. Let compound interest work over time. That's it. Three sentences. Everything else, every course, every guru, every podcast, every book including this one, is commentary on those three sentences.

The reason people keep consuming financial content instead of executing the formula is that execution requires decades of patience, and patience is the cognitive skill human beings are worst at. We are engineered for immediate rewards. Compound interest is the opposite of immediate. It's the slowest, most boring, most relentless force in finance. And it will make you wealthy if you can tolerate the boredom.

The first 13 chapters rebuilt your thinking. This chapter connects that thinking to how money actually works, with specifics I wish someone had given me 15 years ago.

* * *

Three wealth levers. Every financial strategy is a variation of these three.

Lever one: Earned income. Money you trade time for. Salary, hourly wages, freelance fees. The most common lever and the most limited, because there are only so many hours in a day. I spent the first decade of my career focused exclusively on this lever. It built a comfortable life. It could never build wealth on its own. There aren't enough hours.

Lever two: Equity. Ownership. When you own a piece of a business, a property, a stock portfolio, or any asset that grows in value, you're building equity. Equity grows while you sleep. The employee earning $200,000 is doing well. The person who owns 10% of a company valued at $5 million has $500,000 in equity that wasn't earned hour by hour.

Lever three: Leverage. Using borrowed resources to amplify output. A mortgage is leverage: controlling a $400,000 asset with an $80,000 down payment. A business with employees is leverage. Technology is leverage. Content is leverage: create once, generate value for years.

The wealthy understand and combine all three. The middle class typically uses only lever one and wonders why the math never quite works.

* * *

The Cash Flow Quadrant

Robert Kiyosaki's most useful contribution is the Cash Flow Quadrant: four ways to generate income, each with fundamentally different economics.

E (Employee): You work for someone else's system. Income is capped by salary. Time traded hour for hour. Stable. Bounded.

S (Self-Employed): You are the system. Doctors, lawyers, freelancers. You earn more per hour than employees, but if you stop working, income stops. You haven't built a business. You've built a job where you're both the boss and the only employee.

B (Business Owner): You own a system that others operate. Revenue generates whether or not you're present. This is where leverage lives.

I (Investor): Your money works for you. Returns generated by capital, not labor. The endgame.

The critical insight: moving from E to S feels like progress because your hourly rate increases. But it's a lateral move in wealth-building terms because you're still trading time for money. The real transition is from the left side (E and S, where you are the machine) to the right side (B and I, where you own the machine).

* * *

The Slowlane and the Fastlane

MJ DeMarco identifies three financial roadmaps. The Sidewalk: no financial plan, spend everything, hope for a windfall. The Slowlane: good job, save 10%, invest in index funds, retire at 65. The Fastlane: build a scalable business that generates equity and leverage.

The Slowlane is mathematically sound. It's also agonizingly slow and requires betting your financial future on the assumption that nothing disrupts a 40-year plan. In an economy where entire industries can be automated in a decade, that's a bigger gamble than it appears.

Before committing serious time or capital to any Fastlane vehicle, run it through the CENTS filter (Chapter 6). If it fails three or more of the five criteria, it may generate income, but it is unlikely to build wealth.

* * *

The modern vehicles, with the unsexy truths attached.

Traditional employment. The optimization isn't working harder. It's negotiating better (most people leave significant salary on the table), developing premium skills, and maximizing tax-advantaged benefits. If your employer offers a 401(k) match and you're not contributing at least to the match, you're declining free money. I did this for two years early in my career. The compounded cost of those missed contributions makes me wince to calculate.

Investing. For the vast majority of people, the optimal strategy is embarrassingly simple: invest regularly in low-cost, diversified index funds, reinvest dividends, and don't touch it for decades. This strategy outperforms roughly 85% of professional fund managers over any 15-year period. Not because it's clever. Because it's patient.

The math: a person investing $500 per month starting at 25, earning an average 7% annual return, will have approximately $1.2 million by 65. That's $240,000 in contributions and $960,000 in gains. The money you didn't invest made four times more than the money you did. The optimal time to start was 10 years ago. The second-best time is today.

Real estate. One of the most accessible leverage vehicles. A mortgage lets you control an asset worth 5 to 20 times your down payment. But real estate is not passive, no matter what the influencers claim. It involves tenants, maintenance, vacancies, and capital expenditures.

The creator economy. Writing, podcasting, video, courses, newsletters, digital products: content leverage. Create once, generate value indefinitely. Winner-take-most economics, but zero barrier to entry means low experimentation cost.

Entrepreneurship. Highest risk, highest ceiling. Roughly 50% of small businesses fail within five years. The survivors solve genuine problems, achieve product-market fit quickly, and manage cash obsessively.

* * *

Three AI-era wealth applications deserve direct acknowledgment, because they've changed the mechanics of the vehicles above since this advice was last updated.

Robo-advisors and AI investing tools. For the index fund strategy this book recommends, the low-cost, diversified, held-for-decades approach, robo-advisors now execute it competently and at lower cost than most human advisors. Use them for the mechanics. Do not use them to answer the question Chapter 9 asked: what is the money for? That question requires a human with your actual values in the room. Probably you. Definitely not the chatbot.

AI-assisted income streams. AI content generation has flooded the creator economy. The barrier to entry is now essentially zero, which means the barrier to standing out is higher than it has ever been. The skill stack argument from Chapter 4 applies with renewed urgency: the premium goes to work that is specifically, verifiably human in a way the machine cannot replicate.

AI and the E-to-S transition. AI is enabling self-employed workers to operate with business-owner leverage, handling administrative, analytical, and production tasks that previously required employees. For the right person with the right skill stack, this has meaningfully compressed the timeline from the left side of the quadrant to the right. The headcount you used to need to hire, you can now rent by the hour, in tokens.

* * *

What This Looks Like in Your Bank Account: Three Scenarios

Let me make this concrete with three income levels, because abstract principles become useful only when they're specific.

Scenario 1: Making $55,000 per year.

After taxes, you're taking home roughly $3,500 per month. This is tight. The priority is Layer 1 (Defense) and the beginning of Layer 2 (Foundation).

First move: build a $5,000 emergency fund. At $200 per month, that's 25 months. Feels slow. It is slow. But without it, one car repair puts you into debt that compounds against you at 22% interest, which erases months of progress in a single bill.

Second move: if your employer offers a 401(k) match, contribute at least to the match. A typical 50% match on 6% of salary means you contribute $275/month and your employer adds $137.50. That's $137.50 per month in free money. Over 30 years at 7% returns, that employer match alone grows to roughly $170,000. Declining the match is the most expensive financial decision most people make without realizing they're making it.

Third move: eliminate high-interest debt aggressively. Minimum payments on a $5,000 credit card balance at 22% interest cost you roughly $1,100 per year in interest alone. That $1,100, redirected to investing after the debt is paid, compounds to approximately $110,000 over 30 years. Your credit card balance isn't just debt. It's a $110,000 decision you're making every year you carry it.

At $55,000, you're not building a Fastlane business yet. You're building the foundation that makes everything else possible. Layer 1 and early Layer 2. It's not exciting. It's necessary.

Scenario 2: Making $90,000 per year.

After taxes, roughly $5,500 per month. You have breathing room. Layer 1 should be complete or nearly so. The priority shifts to solid Layer 2 and early Layer 3 experiments.

If you can maintain living expenses at $4,000 per month (which requires resisting lifestyle inflation every time your income rises), you have $1,500/month to deploy. Split: $500 to a Roth IRA (maxing it at $6,000/year), $500 to a taxable brokerage account in index funds, and $500 toward a Layer 3 experiment, a side project, a freelance skill, a content platform, whatever your skill stack suggests.

The $500/month in the side project might produce nothing for 12 months. That's fine. You're running an experiment, not betting the farm. The Slowlane ($1,000/month in investments) is running simultaneously. You're on both roads.

At 7% average returns, that $1,000/month in investments alone grows to approximately $1.2 million in 30 years. The side project is your shot at compressing that timeline. If it works, you accelerate. If it doesn't, the Slowlane catches you.

Scenario 3: Making $150,000 per year.

After taxes, roughly $8,500 per month. The danger at this level isn't insufficient income. It's lifestyle inflation. The person making $150,000 who spends $145,000 is in worse financial shape than the person making $70,000 who spends $50,000, because wealth is the gap, not the gross.

If you can hold expenses at $5,500/month (comfortable, not austere), you have $3,000/month to deploy. Max your 401(k) ($23,500/year in 2025). Max your Roth IRA. Open an HSA if you have a high-deductible health plan (triple tax advantage, the most underused account in personal finance). The remainder goes to taxable investments or Layer 3 acceleration.

At this level, you should also be thinking about tax strategy. A good CPA costs $500 to $2,000 per year and typically saves you many multiples of their fee.

Not understanding tax-advantaged accounts at $150,000 is the equivalent of leaving $5,000 to $10,000 on the sidewalk every April.

The real question at $150,000: are you still in the E quadrant or have you started building toward B and I? The income is high enough to fund serious Fastlane experiments without risking financial stability. If you're not experimenting, you're using a $150,000 salary to build a very comfortable Slowlane, which works but wastes the most valuable asset you have at this income level: surplus capital for asymmetric bets.

* * *

Insurance in Plain Language

"Adequate insurance" is a phrase that appears in every financial planning book and is explained in almost none of them. Let me fix that.

Health insurance: non-negotiable. A single hospitalization without insurance can cost $50,000 to $100,000 and will destroy years of financial progress in a single bill. If your employer offers it, take it. If you're self-employed, buy it on the marketplace. The monthly premium feels expensive. The alternative is catastrophic.

Disability insurance: the most underappreciated insurance product in existence. Your ability to earn income is your most valuable financial asset. If you're 30 years old and earning $70,000/year, your future lifetime earnings are roughly $2.8 million. Disability insurance protects that asset. The probability of a working-age adult experiencing a disability lasting 90 days or more before age 65 is approximately 25%. One in four. Those aren't small odds.

Life insurance: necessary if anyone depends on your income. Term life (not whole life, which is an investment product wrapped in insurance clothing and usually benefits the agent more than the policyholder). A healthy 30-year-old can get a $500,000 20-year term policy for roughly $25 to $35 per month. If you have a spouse, children, or anyone who would face financial hardship if you died, this isn't optional.

Liability insurance: if you own a business, a rental property, or significant assets, an umbrella policy ($1 million in additional liability coverage for roughly $200 to $400 per year) is one of the best values in the insurance market.

The principle: insurance protects the foundation layers of the Wealth Stack. Without it, a single adverse event can collapse everything you've built above Layer 1. Insurance isn't exciting. Neither is a building's foundation. Both are the reason the structure above them stays standing.

* * *

Layer 3 Too Early vs. Layer 3 at the Right Time

I want to tell you two stories about the same decision made at different times, because timing is everything in the Wealth Stack.

Story one: a friend of mine quit his job at 28 to start a business. He had no emergency fund, $12,000 in credit card debt, and no savings. His business idea was genuine. His skills were real. His timing was catastrophic. Within four months, a slow client-acquisition period coincided with a car repair and a dental emergency. Without a financial cushion, he funded the gap with more credit card debt. Within eight months, he was $30,000 in debt, stressed beyond function, and took a worse job than the one he'd left just to stabilize. Layer 3 too early. The business might have worked. The foundation wasn't there to support it.

Story two: another friend started the same type of business at 32. She had a six-month emergency fund, zero high-interest debt, and was contributing to her employer's 401(k) up to the match. She built the business on evenings and weekends for 14 months before transitioning to full-time. When the slow acquisition period hit (it always hits), she had the financial cushion to ride it out. She's now four years in, profitable, and building Layer 3 equity on top of a Layer 1 and Layer 2 that never wavered.

Same business model. Same skill level. Same market. Radically different outcomes, determined entirely by whether the Wealth Stack was built in order.

* * *

Savings Rate: The Number That Actually Matters

Your savings rate is your total savings and investments divided by your total after-tax income. It is the single most important number in your financial life, more important than your salary, your investment returns, or your net worth, because it's the only number you can directly control every month.

At a 10% savings rate, you need to work approximately 9 years to save 1 year of living expenses. At a 20% savings rate, 4 years. At 50%, 1 year. The math is nonlinear and counterintuitive: small increases in savings rate produce disproportionate decreases in your working timeline.

The typical American savings rate is approximately 4 to 5%. At that rate, you need to work roughly 19 years to save 1 year of expenses, which means financial independence is mathematically unreachable without significant income increases or investment returns well above historical averages.

Increasing your savings rate from 5% to 20% is not a minor lifestyle adjustment. It's a structural transformation that will compress your timeline to financial independence by decades. And it's achievable for most people in the $55,000-plus range through a combination of expense reduction and income growth, not through deprivation but through the lifestyle design we covered in Chapter 9. When you've defined what enough actually costs, you stop spending on the things that were never part of the plan.

* * *

The Wealth Stack: Build in Order

Layer 1: Defense. Emergency fund (3 to 6 months of expenses), adequate insurance, high-interest debt eliminated. This layer doesn't make you wealthy. It prevents you from being destroyed. Build it first.

Layer 2: Foundation. Employer retirement match captured, consistent index fund investing (even

$100/month), basic tax optimization. Boring. Supposed to be. Boring is what compounding looks like from the inside.

Layer 3: Acceleration. Multiple income streams (designed using the Revenue Architecture from Chapter 6) skill-stack monetization, equity investments, business building. Earned income converting to equity. More risk, more sophistication, more upside. Only build here when Layers 1 and 2 are solid.

Layer 4: Optimization. Tax strategy with a professional, estate planning, philanthropy, legacy. Only matters after Layers 1 through 3 are solid.

Kiyosaki tells you where to go (left side to right side of the quadrant). DeMarco tells you how fast you can get there (Slowlane vs Fastlane). The Wealth Stack tells you what order to build in so the structure holds.

* * *

The Wealth Stack Assessment: This Week's Challenge

Assess each layer with brutal honesty. No aspirational answers.

Layer 1: Do you have 3 to 6 months of expenses saved? Is high-interest debt eliminated? Do you have health, disability, and life insurance (if dependents)? If any answer is no, this is your priority. Not Layer 2. Not Layer 3. This.

Layer 2: Are you capturing your full employer match? Are you investing consistently? Do you understand 401(k), Roth IRA, and HSA? If not, 30 minutes this week. Set up or increase automatic contributions.

Layer 3: If Layers 1 and 2 are solid, what is your best Fastlane vehicle? Run it through the CENTS filter (Chapter 6) before committing. Then build a 90-day sprint.

Calculate your savings rate right now. Below 10%: emergency mode. 10 to 15%: functional. 15 to 25%: strong. Above 25%: you're compressing the timeline.

Identify which quadrant you're currently in (E, S, B, or I). Write down what a move one quadrant to the right would look like. What skills, systems, or structures would it require? That's your Layer 3 design target.

The money mechanics are not complicated. They're boring, specific, and relentless. The thinking was the first 13 chapters. This is the plumbing. Neither works alone. Together, they're a system.

CHAPTER 15

The Anti-Guru: Why Most Financial Advice

Is Designed to Sell You Something

There is a man on YouTube right now, recording a video in front of a rented Lamborghini, telling you that he can teach you to make $10,000 per month in passive income if you join his mentorship program for $1,997. His program has 47 modules, a private Discord server, and weekly group coaching calls. His testimonials feature people holding oversized checks. His content is free, generous, and relentless. He posts three times a day. He seems genuine. He seems successful. He seems like he wants to help you.

He is selling you. Everything he does, every video, every podcast, every free PDF, every inspirational Instagram story, is a conversion funnel designed to move you from viewer to customer. The Lamborghini is a prop. The testimonials are cherry-picked from thousands of students, most of whom made nothing. The "passive income" he teaches generates passive income for exactly one person: him, through course sales.

I'm not saying he's a bad person. He might genuinely believe he's helping. But his business model has a structural conflict of interest that makes his advice unreliable, and understanding that conflict is one of the most financially valuable skills you can develop.

* * *

The financial advice industry has a problem that nobody in the industry wants to talk about: the people giving advice make their money from giving advice, not from following it.

This isn't universally true. Some financial advisors eat their own cooking. Some authors practice what they preach. But the incentive structure of the modern advice economy, particularly on YouTube, Instagram, TikTok, and the podcast circuit, is built on a model where the advice itself is the product, and the quality of the advice is secondary to its ability to generate engagement, leads, and sales.

Let me walk you through the economics, because once you see the machine, you can never unsee it.

A YouTube channel about personal finance generates revenue from three sources. First, ad revenue, which pays roughly $5 to $15 per thousand views depending on the niche. A video with 100,000 views might earn $500 to $1,500 in ad revenue. Decent, but not life-changing. Second, sponsorships, which pay $5,000 to $50,000 per video for established channels. This is where the money starts. Third, product sales: courses, coaching, masterminds, membership communities. This is where the real money lives. A single course priced at $997 with 200 students per launch generates $199,400 per launch. Run four launches per year and you're approaching a million dollars in revenue.

Now ask yourself: if your income depends on selling a course, what kind of advice are you incentivized to give? The kind that solves the viewer's problem so completely they never need to buy anything? Or the kind that creates enough value to establish trust but leaves enough gaps that the viewer feels they need more, more that conveniently comes in the form of your $997 program?

The answer is obvious. And it's not malicious. It's structural. The business model rewards creating dependency, not independence. The best possible outcome for the advice-giver is a customer who keeps coming back: upgrading to the premium tier, joining the mastermind, attending the live event, buying the next course. The best possible outcome for the advice-receiver is learning enough to never need the advice-giver again. These two outcomes are in direct tension.

This is the fundamental conflict of interest at the heart of the modern financial advice economy, and almost nobody talks about it because the people with the largest platforms are the ones benefiting from the conflict.

* * *

Here's a quick taxonomy of the most common guru business models, so you can recognize them in the wild.

The Aspiration Seller. Leads with lifestyle: the car, the house, the travel, the freedom. The implicit promise is "buy my program and you'll live like me." The implicit omission is that they live like that because they sell programs, not because the strategies in their programs work. Their wealth comes from teaching, not doing. This isn't inherently wrong. Teaching is a legitimate business. But when the teacher implies their wealth comes from the strategy they're teaching rather than from selling the strategy, that's a material misrepresentation.

The Complexity Creator. Makes simple concepts sound difficult so that you feel you need expert guidance. Investing in index funds is a boring, four-sentence strategy. But boring doesn't sell courses. So the Complexity Creator introduces options strategies, sector rotation, technical analysis, crypto yield farming, and synthetic derivatives until you're so overwhelmed that paying $497 for their "Simplified System" feels like a bargain. The irony: the best financial strategy for most people is the boring one. The course exists to justify its own existence.

The Community Builder. Creates a paid membership community where the primary value is access to other members who are also trying to figure things out. The guru's contribution is a weekly call and occasional content drops. The price is $49 to $299 per month. The value proposition is belonging, which is real and legitimate, but it's being sold as financial education, which it often isn't. You're paying for a peer group. There's nothing wrong with that, but call it what it is.

The Certification Mill. Sells you a credential that they invented, which is recognized only by other people who bought the same credential from the same person. "Become a Certified Wealth Mindset Coach!" The certification costs $3,000 to $10,000. It qualifies you for nothing in the regulated financial industry. What it qualifies you for is selling the same certification to other aspiring coaches, creating a multi-level structure that would make Amway blush.

The Free-to-Paid Pipeline. Gives away genuinely useful free content (YouTube videos, podcasts, email newsletters) that builds trust and establishes expertise. Then offers a paid product that promises to go "deeper." The free content is the hook. The paid product is the catch. This model is the most defensible of the bunch because the free content often has real value. The question to ask: does the paid product deliver value proportional to its price, or does it primarily deliver access to the same person who was free last week?

* * *

I want to be clear about something: not all paid financial education is a scam. Some courses are excellent. Some coaches are transformative. Some communities are genuinely worth the membership fee. The existence of bad actors doesn't invalidate the entire ecosystem any more than the existence of bad restaurants invalidates the concept of eating out.

The skill you need isn't cynicism. It's discernment. And discernment requires a framework.

Here's the BS Detection Framework I use to evaluate any piece of financial advice before I act on it or pay for it. Five questions. Takes about two minutes. Has saved me thousands of dollars and an immeasurable amount of wasted time.

* * *

Question one: How does this person make their money? If a real estate guru makes their money from real estate, their advice has at least passed the basic credibility test. If a real estate guru makes their money from selling courses about real estate, the advice is marketing material, not market intelligence. Follow the revenue. Always follow the revenue.

Question two: What are the base rates? If someone claims their students achieve extraordinary results, ask what percentage of students achieve those results. A program that produces five success stories out of 5,000 students has a success rate of 0.1%. Those five testimonials are real. They're also statistically meaningless. Base rates are the antidote to testimonial cherry-picking.

Question three: Is the advice actionable without further purchase? If the free advice creates a clear next step you can execute independently, it's probably genuine education. If the free advice creates a clear next step that requires buying the paid product, it's a sales funnel. Good education makes you more independent. Good marketing makes you more dependent.

Question four: Does the advice acknowledge trade-offs and risks? Real financial knowledge is full of trade-offs, uncertainties, and "it depends." If someone presents a strategy as all upside with no downside, they're either lying or they don't understand the strategy well enough to teach it. Sophistication sounds like "here are the conditions under which this works and the conditions under which it doesn't." Selling sounds like "this always works."

Question five: Would this person give me this advice if they couldn't profit from it? Imagine the guru at a dinner party, no cameras, no sales page, no affiliate links. Would they tell their actual friend to do what they're telling you to do? If you can't imagine them giving the same advice with zero financial incentive, the advice is contaminated by the business model.

* * *

The Funnel Behind the Free Content

Let me show you exactly how the free-to-paid pipeline works so you can recognize it in real time.

Stage one: The Hook. A short, high-value video or article that solves a real problem. This is genuinely useful content, and that's what makes it effective. The guru isn't lying at this stage. They're investing. The free content costs them time and production resources, and they recoup it downstream.

Stage two: The Nurture. More free content, usually via email newsletter. Each email provides value but also subtly establishes the guru's authority and creates a sense of relationship. You start to feel like you know them. You trust them. They understand your situation.

Stage three: The Pivot. A piece of content that describes a problem the free content can't fully solve. "I've given you the foundation, but to go deeper, you need the full framework." This is the bridge between free and paid. The problem is real. The solution is real. But the framing implies that you need the paid product to complete what the free content started.

Stage four: The Launch. A time-limited offer with urgency mechanics: countdown timers, limited spots, bonus packages that expire, testimonials from early adopters. The scarcity is usually manufactured. The bonuses are repackaged existing content. The testimonials are real but statistically unrepresentative.

Stage five: The Upsell. After purchase, you're offered the premium tier: group coaching, one-on-one access, a mastermind, an inner circle. Each tier costs more and promises closer proximity to the guru.

None of this is illegal. Most of it isn't even unethical in isolation. The question is whether the value at each stage justifies the price, and whether the structure is designed to solve your problem or to maximize your lifetime customer value. Those are different objectives, and the guru's business model is optimized for the second one.

The BS Detection Framework from earlier in this chapter applies at every stage. Follow the revenue. Check the base rates. Test whether the advice is actionable independently. Look for acknowledged trade-offs. And ask whether the person would give you this advice at a dinner party with no cameras running.

* * *

Everything I just described is getting harder to evaluate, because the person delivering the financial advice may not be a person.

AI-generated financial content is here. Synthetic voices, AI-written scripts, algorithmically optimized video content, deepfake presenters. As of 2026, most of it is indistinguishable from human-authored material to the average viewer. The conflict-of-interest analysis above still applies, but you now need an additional filter before you even run it: is there a human being with genuine financial experience and genuine accountability behind this content, or is this AI-optimized output engineered to maximize watch time regardless of whether the advice is sound? In other words: is there a person whose name you could subpoena, or just a brand name and a thumbnail?

The economics are straightforward. AI allows anyone to produce financial content at industrial scale with no expertise required. A motivated operator with a $50-per-month model subscription can now generate the equivalent of 40 hours of financial education content per week. Some of that content will be accurate. Much of it will be confident-sounding and wrong. None of the operators will be available when the advice turns out to be bad. They will be making the next channel.

The existing BS Detection Framework handles this: follow the revenue, check the base rates, test whether the advice is actionable independently. But add one more question for the AI era: is there a named, verifiable human being who stands behind this advice and whose reputation would suffer if it's wrong? If not, the accountability structure that makes advice trustworthy doesn't exist.

Content without human accountability is not education. It is content.

* * *

Why "Just Google It" Isn't the Answer Either

I've spent this chapter critiquing the guru economy, and I want to be honest about the alternative: free information isn't automatically better than paid information. Google will give you 50 contradictory answers to any financial question. Reddit will give you 50 more, most of them from anonymous strangers whose credentials are unverifiable and whose incentives are unclear.

The value of a well-constructed book, course, or program isn't the information. It's the curation, the sequencing, and the framework. The same information arranged in a thoughtful sequence by someone who understands how learning actually works (hello, instructional designer here) produces dramatically better outcomes than the same information scattered across 200 blog posts in random order.

The distinction isn't paid versus free. It's engineered-to-teach versus engineered-to-sell. This book is engineered to teach. It's organized around a learning framework (the Think Again Loop) based on decades of instructional design research. The exercises are sequenced to build on each other. The concepts are scaffolded so that each chapter uses vocabulary and frameworks established in previous chapters.

That's not an accident. That's design. And good design, whether in a book, a course, or a coaching program, is worth paying for. The test isn't whether someone charges money. The test is whether the product is built around your learning outcomes or their revenue outcomes.

If you can answer that question honestly, you don't need this chapter. You already have the most valuable filter in the modern information economy: the ability to distinguish between someone who wants to teach you and someone who wants to sell you.

* * *

Let me apply this framework to the books I've drawn from throughout Think Again, because I believe in turning the lens on my own sources.

Napoleon Hill: made his money from book sales and speaking, not from the business strategies he described. Many of his claimed interviews have never been verified. His personal financial history was turbulent. Credibility: the principles have been validated by subsequent research, but Hill himself is more philosopher than practitioner. Take the ideas. Verify independently.

Robert Kiyosaki: the Cash Flow Quadrant is genuinely useful (and appears in Chapter 14 of this book). But Kiyosaki's specific investment advice has been widely criticized for oversimplification, and his "Rich Dad" may be a composite or fictional character. His primary income comes from books and seminars, not from the real estate and business strategies he teaches. Take the frameworks. Ignore the specific investment advice. Verify everything.

MJ DeMarco: the CENTS framework (Chapter 6 and 14) is one of the most useful business evaluation tools I've encountered. DeMarco actually built and sold businesses before writing about them. Higher credibility on the practitioner test. His aggressive tone and "everyone else is an idiot" positioning should be taken with appropriate salt.

Tim Ferriss: Dreamlining and Fear-Setting (Chapters 7 and 9) are useful exercises. Ferriss's business advice is informed by actual entrepreneurial experience. His lifestyle claims have been questioned but his frameworks are practical and testable. Moderate-to-high credibility.

T. Harv Eker: the Financial Thermostat (Chapter 3) maps onto neuroscience whether Eker intended it to or not. His primary business, however, is seminars and courses, and his events use high-pressure upselling tactics that should make anyone cautious. Take the thermostat concept. Skip the seminar.

I've tried to be honest about every source I've used in this book. Some are stronger than others. None are infallible. And the willingness to evaluate your own sources, to apply the same critical framework to the people you agree with as the people you don't, is the final layer of financial sophistication.

* * *

The deeper issue beneath the guru economy is this: we want someone to tell us what to do.

Building wealth is uncertain. The variables are complex. The timeline is long. The feedback loops are slow. And in the face of all that uncertainty, the human brain craves a confident voice that says, "Do this and it will work." The guru fills that craving. The guru reduces complexity to simplicity, uncertainty to confidence, and a ten-year process to a five-step system.

The problem isn't that simplification is wrong. This entire book is a simplification. Every framework, every model, every principle is a reduction of complex reality into something manageable. The problem is when simplification is sold as completeness, when the guru implies that their five-step system captures the full complexity of building wealth and that failure to achieve results means you didn't follow the steps, not that the steps were incomplete.

The antidote to guru dependency is the same thing this entire book has been building: a personal operating system for financial decision-making that doesn't require an external authority to function. When you can examine your own defaults, design your own systems, execute with your own feedback loops, and recalibrate based on your own evidence, you don't need a guru. You need data, a framework, and the willingness to iterate.

You already have the framework. It's in the previous 14 chapters.

The data comes from your own life, your own numbers, your own experiments.

The willingness to iterate comes from you.

Nobody can sell you that. And that's exactly why it's valuable.

* * *

One final thought, and I'll let you go.

This book costs whatever you paid for it. There is no upsell. There is no $1,997 mastermind. There is no private Discord server. There is no weekly coaching call. There is no certification. There is no premium tier.

If this book helped you, the only thing I'd ask is that you apply the exercises, track your results, and share the book with someone who needs it. Not because I need the sales (though I appreciate them). Because the best financial education spreads peer to peer, not guru to followcr.

The person you trust most with financial advice shouldn't be me. It shouldn't be any author, YouTuber, or podcast host. It should be the version of yourself that emerges after you've done the work in these pages: examined, designed, executed, and recalibrated.

That person doesn't need a guru.

That person is the guru.

Now go prove it.

One Year from Now

I want to leave you with a specific image. Not a visualization exercise. Something concrete.

One year from now, you will be sitting somewhere, probably the same place you're sitting right now, and you'll be either the person who read this book and did the exercises, or the person who read this book and didn't.

The person who did the exercises has a different net worth calculation, not because of magic but because they looked at their actual numbers and closed the gaps they found. They have a skill stack they've deliberately advanced. They have implementation intentions running quietly in the background, catching impulse purchases and redirecting financial energy. They have a 90-day sprint behind them that produced measurable results. They have a Master Mind group that holds them accountable. They have a decision journal with three months of entries showing their bias patterns. They know their freedom number. They know their thermostat setting. And they've started moving both.

The person who didn't do the exercises is the same person they were when they opened the book. Slightly more informed. Slightly more aware. But fundamentally unchanged, because knowledge without application is just entertainment with footnotes.

I can't make you do the work. No book can. But I can tell you, from the trail, that the work works. Not perfectly. Not immediately. Not without setbacks, embarrassments, and the occasional parking-lot crisis. But it works.

The Think Again Loop doesn't promise a destination. It promises a process: examine, design, execute, recalibrate. Run the loop. Run it again. Get better at running it. The wealth follows the improvement, not the other way around.

APPENDIX

The Think Again Toolkit

You're still here.

Fifteen chapters. Thirteen principles rebuilt from the studs. Two bridge chapters where I asked you to stop chasing and start thinking about what you're actually building. One appendix that collects every exercise so you can find them without flipping through 200 pages. And a fair number of jokes, not all of which landed, but I respect your patience with the ones that didn't.

Before the summary, something Hill didn't say in his conclusion: what this book cannot do.

It cannot guarantee wealth. No book can, and any book claiming otherwise has confused confidence with honesty. It cannot erase systemic barriers or bad luck or the thousand variables of a human life that no framework can predict. It cannot replace the work.

It can only make the work smarter.

What it can do is replace unexamined defaults with deliberate choices. That sentence is the entire book compressed to 10 words. Every chapter attacked a default that was costing you money, time, or cognitive capacity, and replaced it with something better.

* * *

The 13 principles, rebuilt. Your reference card.

1. Directed Desire.

Define what you want in operational terms with numbers, timelines, and vehicles. Use WOOP to identify internal obstacles. Create implementation intentions. Audit your dopamine diet. Look at your actual numbers. Revisit every 90 days.

2. Calibrated Confidence.

Build self-efficacy through mastery experiences and credible feedback. Detect impostor syndrome and Dunning-Kruger in yourself. Use CBT to rewrite undermining beliefs with evidence-based alternatives.

3. Evidence-Based Reprogramming.

Use third-person self-talk, behavioral evidence stacking, and habit stacking. Protect your inputs from algorithmic narrative machines. Rewrite money stories with evidence, not affirmation.

4. Applied Specialized Knowledge.

Practice deliberately, targeting weaknesses with feedback. Build a skill stack that creates unique value. Prioritize deep work. Use AI as a tool; your judgment is the asset.

5. Combinatorial Imagination.

Consume widely, create constraints, schedule incubation. Use the Collision Method. In an age of machine-generated competence, original human thinking is the premium asset.

6. Systems Over Goals.

Set direction with OKRs. Build daily systems. Run Pre-Mortems. Design your Revenue Architecture. Iterate in 90-day sprints.

7. Decisive Action.

Reduce decision volume to protect decision quality. Classify as Type 1 or Type 2. Decide at 70% information for reversible choices. Speed of learning beats perfection of any single choice.

8. Strategic Persistence.

Define Kill Criteria before you start. Apply the Fresh Eyes Test. Read the trend. Know the difference between productive persistence, sunk-cost stubbornness, and strategic pivoting.

9. Define Enough.

Design your ideal ordinary Tuesday. Calculate your freedom number. Make sure the money serves the life, not the reverse.

10. Strategic Relationships.

Build a Master Mind for depth. Maintain weak ties for breadth. Be a strategic giver. Filter ruthlessly for takers.

11. Energy Management.

Protect sleep. Work in 90-minute cycles. Exercise as cognitive infrastructure. Conduct periodic dopamine resets. Output quality is bounded by energy quality.

12. Cognitive Sovereignty.

Learn the biases that cost you the most. Build a latticework of mental models. Keep a decision journal. Seek disconfirming evidence as a discipline.

13. Calibrated Intuition.

Trust your gut when you're experienced, the domain is patterned, and you're calm. Question it when you're a novice, the situation is novel, or your emotions are steering. Build a personal accuracy database.

* * *

The throughline across all 13: every principle replaces an unexamined default with a deliberate choice.

Your default desires were vague. We made them operational.

Your default confidence was miscalibrated. We gave it a ruler.

Your default narratives were inherited. We rebuilt them from evidence.

Your default knowledge was passive. We put it to work.

Your default creativity was dormant. We woke it up.

Your default planning was wishful. We gave it an engine.

Your default decisions were fatigued. We cleared the noise.

Your default persistence was blind. We gave it vision.

Your default definition of wealth was someone else's. We made it yours.

Your default relationships were accidental. We made them intentional.

Your default energy was leaking. We plugged the holes.

Your default thinking was biased. We installed lenses.

Your default intuition was untested. We built a scorecard.

* * *

I want to close with something I almost left out because it's vulnerable and I've spent 15 chapters performing competence. But competence without honesty is just a shinier version of the self-help industry I've been criticizing, and I'd rather end honestly than polished.

I didn't write this book because I've arrived. I wrote it because I'm building. The principles in these pages are principles I use, not principles I've transcended. I still catch myself avoiding decisions. I still notice my confirmation bias mid-sentence. I still reach for my phone when I should be reaching for a harder thought. I still occasionally fantasize about outcomes instead of planning for obstacles.

The difference between now and a decade ago isn't that I've conquered these patterns. It's that I can see them. And seeing them, naming them, building systems to counteract them, measuring the results, and adjusting, that's the whole game. Not perfection. Awareness plus iteration.

Building wealth in the modern world is harder than it's ever been and more possible than it's ever been. The barriers are higher and the tools are better. The economy is less forgiving and the information is more accessible. Both things, simultaneously. The people who build are the ones who can hold both truths at once without being paralyzed by either.

I hope this book gave you better tools. More than that, I hope it gave you the feeling that someone is in your corner who isn't trying to sell you a course, who isn't performing guru energy from a rented mansion, who is just a person with too many degrees and a deep conviction that you can build the financial life you want if you're willing to think clearly, act strategically, and treat yourself with the same compassion you'd give a friend.

Napoleon Hill said to think and grow rich.

I'm asking you to think again... in a loop.

* * *

Every exercise from the book, collected in one place. Each is designed to be completed in one sitting or one week. Do them in order if you're methodical. Cherry-pick if you're impatient. But do them. Reading about financial psychology without doing the exercises is like reading a cookbook and calling it dinner.

* * *

1. The Desire Audit (Chapter 1)

Define your 12-month financial target as a specific number. Identify the real "why" underneath the surface answer. Name your primary internal obstacle. Write three implementation intentions (if X, then Y). List your top three dopamine drains with a reduction plan. Check your actual financial numbers: net worth, savings rate, total debt.

2. The Confidence Calibration (Chapter 2)

Pick your most important financial goal. Rate competence (1-10) using evidence. Rate confidence (1-10) using gut feel. If competence \\> confidence: build an evidence file. If confidence \\> competence: seek honest external feedback. Identify one undermining belief and rewrite it using the CBT filter.

3. The Narrative Rewrite (Chapter 3)

Write three deep money stories you carry. Find three pieces of contradicting evidence for each from your own life. Write a replacement narrative anchored in present action, not future fantasy. Reinforce daily using third-person self-talk.

4. The Skill Stack Audit (Chapter 4)

List every skill at 6/10 or higher. Circle three that create the most unique intersection. Rate each level and identify one advancement action with a deliverable and 90-day deadline. Identify one gap skill. Build one daily 90-minute deep work block.

5. The Collision Method (Chapter 5)

Weekly: two random Wikipedia articles, 15-minute timer, ten forced connections. Circle the most surprising. Develop it for five more minutes. Keep a log. Watch for involuntary pattern-matching emerging within two months.

6. The 90-Day Sprint (Chapter 6)

One Objective. Three measurable Key Results. Design the daily system with uncomfortable specificity. Run a Pre-Mortem. Assess your Revenue Architecture (Foundation, Growth, Passive, Insurance). Schedule a 15-minute weekly review every Sunday.

7. The Decision Diet (Chapter 7)

Day 1-2: Track and categorize every decision as High or Low Impact. Days 3-5: Eliminate or automate five Low Impact decisions. Days 6-7: Identify and resolve the one big decision you've been avoiding. Classify it as Type 1 or Type 2 and act accordingly.

8. The Quit Criteria Checklist (Chapter 8)

Define the venture in one sentence. Set three specific Kill Criteria with deadlines. Apply the Fresh Eyes Test. Assess the trend (improving, flat, declining). Check your identity attachment and rewrite at one level higher. Share with a truth-teller.

9. The Enough Exercise (Chapter 9)

Describe your ideal ordinary Tuesday in detail. Cost it out precisely. Calculate your freedom number (annual cost / 0.04). Calculate your current gap and timeline. Answer: if you had enough tomorrow, what would you do with your time?

10. The Inner Circle Audit (Chapter 10)

List the five people you spend the most professional time with. Assess each: challenge or agree? Complement or duplicate? Giver, matcher, or taker? Identify the gap in your circle. List three people who could fill it. Reach out to one this week.

11. The Energy Audit (Chapter 11)

Seven days: rate energy 1-10 three times daily. Log sleep, exercise, screen time, and primary activity. Find patterns. Protect your peak window for deep work. Add one exercise session. Set a daily screen time limit.

12. The Two-Part Mind-Brain Audit (Chapter 12)

Part A. The Bias Audit (15 minutes): Review your last three significant financial decisions. Identify active biases. Apply three mental models to your weakest decision. Identify your dominant bias. Start a decision journal: decision, reasoning, expected outcome, suspected biases, date. Review quarterly.

Part B. The Digital Detox Protocol (7 days): Day 1: Measure screen time and daily pickups. Day 2: Add friction to your top three high-consumption apps. Day 3: Install 60-minute morning and evening screen blackouts. Days 4 through 6: One 90-minute deep work block daily with phone in another room. Day 7: Measure again and compare.

13. The Gut-Check Journal (Chapter 13)

Two weeks: record gut feeling before every financial decision. Record the decision and outcome. Calculate gut accuracy by domain. Identify where your intuition is reliable and where it runs on emotion instead of experience.

14. The Wealth Stack Assessment (Chapter 14)

Assess each layer: Defense (emergency fund, insurance, debt), Foundation (retirement match, index investing, tax basics), Acceleration (multiple income streams, equity building), Optimization (tax strategy, estate planning). Build in order. Calculate savings rate. Write your timeline to the crossover point.

* * *

Recommended Reading

Thinking, Fast and Slow by Daniel Kahneman. Atomic Habits by James Clear. The Psychology of Money by Morgan Housel. Deep Work by Cal Newport. Grit by Angela Duckworth. Thinking in Bets and Quit by Annie Duke. Flow by Mihaly Csikszentmihalyi. Why We Sleep by Matthew

Walker. Give and Take by Adam Grant. Dopamine Nation by Anna Lembke. Chatter by Ethan Kross. The Brain That Changes Itself by Norman Doidge. Measure What Matters by John Doerr. Sources of Power by Gary Klein. Clear Thinking by Shane Parrish. Your Money or Your Life by Vicki Robin. Rethinking Positive Thinking by Gabriele Oettingen. The Paradox of Choice by Barry Schwartz. Spark by John Ratey. Risk Savvy by Gerd Gigerenzer. Scott Adams' How to Fail at Almost Everything and Still Win Big.

* * *

Thank you for reading Think Again Loop.

Now close the book and go build something.

GLOSSARY

Key Terms, Theories, and Frameworks

Anchoring Bias. The tendency for the first number you encounter in a decision to disproportionately influence all subsequent judgments. In salary negotiations, the person who states a number first sets the anchor. In purchasing, the first price you see becomes the reference point against which all other prices are evaluated, regardless of whether that first price was rational. (Chapter 12)

Autosuggestion. Napoleon Hill's term for the practice of feeding specific thoughts to the subconscious mind through repeated verbal and emotional emphasis. Modernized in this book as evidence-based reprogramming through self-distanced self-talk, behavioral evidence stacking, and habit stacking. (Chapter 3)

Behavioral Evidence Stacking. The practice of deliberately creating small actions that serve as evidence for the financial identity you are building. Each action (automating a savings transfer, negotiating a bill, tracking expenses) sends a signal to your subconscious that reinforces the new identity. Derived from James Clear's identity-based habit framework. (Chapter 3)

CENTS Framework. MJ DeMarco's filter for evaluating whether a business venture can build real wealth: Control (do you own the key variables?), Entry barriers (can competitors easily replicate you?), Need (does it solve a real problem people pay for?), Time-independence (does it run without your hour-by-hour involvement?), Scale (can it serve 10x more customers without 10x more effort?). (Chapters 6)

Cash Flow Quadrant. Robert Kiyosaki's model of four income types: E (Employee), S (Self-Employed), B (Business Owner), I (Investor). The critical insight is that moving from E to S is a lateral move in wealth-building terms because both trade time for money. The real transition is from the left side (E/S) to the right side (B/I), where you own the system rather than being the system. (Chapter 15)

Cognitive Bias. A systematic pattern of deviation from rational judgment. Over 180 cognitive biases have been documented. The five most financially expensive are confirmation bias, anchoring bias, loss aversion, the availability heuristic, and status quo bias. Biases cannot be eliminated but can be partially mitigated through awareness, mental models, and structured decision processes. (Chapter 12)

Combinatorial Creativity. The ability to connect ideas from unrelated domains to produce something new and useful. Also called bisociation (Arthur Koestler). The Collision Method exercise trains this ability. In the AI era, combinatorial creativity is the primary human advantage over machine-generated output. (Chapter 5)

Compound Interest. The process by which investment returns generate their own returns over time. A person investing $500/month at 7% annual return from age 25 will have approximately $1.2 million by age 65, of which $960,000 is gains rather than contributions. Often described as the most powerful force in finance. Its primary requirement is time. (Chapter 15)

Crossover Point. The moment when investment income exceeds living expenses, making paid work optional. Calculated by dividing annual expenses by 0.04 (the 4% withdrawal rate). This is the numerical definition of financial independence. (Chapter 9)

Decision Fatigue. Roy Baumeister's finding that every decision you make draws from the same finite pool of cognitive resources. The pool depletes throughout the day, leading to worse decisions or decision avoidance by evening. The antidote is reducing total decision volume through automation and elimination of low-impact choices. (Chapter 7)

Deep Work. Cal Newport's term for cognitively demanding, distraction-free concentration that produces real output. Research shows it takes 23 minutes to fully re-engage after an interruption. Two to three hours of genuine deep work per day outproduces most people's eight-hour fragmented workdays. (Chapter 4)

Deliberate Practice. Anders Ericsson's framework for skill development: target specific weaknesses, obtain immediate feedback, operate at the edge of your ability, and sustain mental exhaustion. Limited to approximately four hours per day even for elite performers. Distinct from ordinary practice, which reinforces existing strengths. (Chapter 4)

Directed Desire. This book's modernization of Hill's first principle. Desire defined in operational terms (specific amount, timeline, and vehicle) combined with obstacle awareness (WOOP), implementation intentions, dopamine management, and 90-day recalibration cycles. (Chapter 1)

Dopamine. A neurotransmitter associated with anticipation and motivation, not pleasure. Released in response to predicted rewards, not actual rewards. Chronic digital overstimulation downregulates dopamine receptors, making effortful activities feel less rewarding. Managed through periodic dopamine fasting and deliberate reduction of high-stimulation inputs. (Chapters 1, 11, 12)

Dunning-Kruger Effect. The tendency for people with low competence in a domain to dramatically overestimate their ability, precisely because they lack the knowledge to recognize their own ignorance. The inverse of impostor syndrome. Particularly dangerous in investing, where overconfident beginners often underperform passive strategies. (Chapters 2, 12)

Financial Thermostat. T. Harv Eker's concept of an unconscious wealth set point. Your subconscious maintains a specific financial identity and generates sabotaging behaviors (impulsive spending, underearning, self-undermining) whenever your actual wealth deviates too far from the set point. Recalibrated through behavioral evidence stacking and neuroplasticity. (Chapters 3, 12)

Flow State. Mihaly Csikszentmihalyi's term for complete absorption in a task where time distorts, self-consciousness disappears, and performance peaks. Requires clear goals, immediate feedback, challenge matched to skill level, and freedom from distraction. Produces the highest-quality cognitive output. (Chapter 11)

Freedom Number. The investment portfolio size needed to fund your ideal lifestyle indefinitely at a 4% annual withdrawal rate. Calculated as annual living expenses divided by 0.04. Represents the concrete financial target derived from the Enough Exercise. (Chapter 9)

Growth Mindset. Carol Dweck's finding that people who believe abilities are developable through effort and strategy outperform those who believe abilities are fixed. Does not mean "you can do anything." Means your limits are further out than you think and can be expanded through strategy and feedback. (Chapter 2)

Implementation Intention. Peter Gollwitzer's technique of linking specific situations to specific actions using if-then format. People who form these intentions are two to three times more likely to follow through than those who merely set goals. Removes negotiation from the moment of action. (Chapter 1)

Kill Criteria. Pre-defined, specific, measurable conditions under which you will walk away from a venture. Set before emotional investment begins, when rational assessment is still possible. Prevents sunk-cost persistence by making the quit decision in advance. (Chapter 8)

Loss Aversion. Daniel Kahneman and Amos Tversky's finding that losing $100 feels approximately twice as painful as gaining $100 feels good. Produces irrational financial behavior: holding losing investments too long, selling winners too early, and passing on reasonable opportunities because potential losses loom larger than potential gains. (Chapter 12)

Master Mind. Napoleon Hill's concept of a small, committed, trust-based alliance of people working toward compatible goals. Modernized as three to five cognitively diverse individuals meeting biweekly with structured accountability. Distinguished from networking by depth of trust and specificity of shared purpose. (Chapter 10)

Mental Models. Charlie Munger's latticework of frameworks from multiple disciplines used to improve decision-making. Key models include inversion (how would I guarantee failure?), second-order thinking (and then what?), circle of competence (where am I qualified?), margin of safety (what buffer exists?), and map versus territory (is my model accurate?). (Chapter 12)

Neuroplasticity. The brain's ability to physically reorganize itself by forming new neural connections throughout life. The scientific basis for Hill's principle that thoughts shape reality. Neurons that fire together wire together: repeated thoughts and behaviors strengthen associated pathways while unused pathways weaken. (Chapters 3, 12)

OODA Loop. John Boyd's decision cycle: Observe, Orient, Decide, Act. The side that cycles through this loop faster wins, because faster iteration produces faster learning. Applied to wealth-building: speed of decision and iteration matters more than perfection of any single choice. (Chapter 7)

Revenue Architecture. This book's framework for structuring multiple income streams: Foundation Income (primary job, stability), Growth Income (side project, higher ceiling), Passive Income (investments, royalties, compounds over time), and Insurance Income (emergency fallback skill). (Chapter 6)

Reticular Activating System (RAS). A neural filter at the base of the brainstem that selects which 50 bits of the 11 million bits of sensory information per second reach conscious awareness. Selected for relevance, novelty, and emotional significance. When you define a clear financial goal, your RAS begins filtering the world for related opportunities. (Chapter 12)

Self-Efficacy. Albert Bandura's concept of believing in your ability to execute specific behaviors in specific situations to produce specific outcomes. Built from four sources: mastery experiences, vicarious experience, verbal persuasion, and physiological state. Distinguished from vague "self-confidence" by its specificity and evidence base. (Chapter 2)

Skill Stack. Scott Adams's concept of combining two to three complementary skills at the top-25% level to create a unique value proposition. Being world-class at one skill is extraordinarily difficult. Being good at three complementary skills creates an intersection where competition is thin and value is high. (Chapter 4)

Sunk Cost Fallacy. The tendency to continue investing in something because of what you have already invested, rather than based on future expected returns. Past investments are gone regardless of future decisions. Every additional dollar spent on a losing venture is a new loss, not a recovery of old ones. (Chapter 8)

The Think Again Loop. This book's signature framework: a four-phase cycle of Examine (audit your defaults), Design (build your system), Execute (act with feedback), and Recalibrate (update based on evidence). Runs on a 90-day cadence. Wealth is built through iterative loops, not single passes. (Throughout)

Wealth Stack. This book's four-layer framework for building financial security in order: Layer 1 Defense (emergency fund, insurance, debt elimination),

Layer 2 Foundation (retirement match, index investing, tax optimization), Layer 3 Acceleration (multiple income streams, equity building, business), Layer 4 Optimization (tax strategy, estate planning, legacy). Must be built in sequence. (Chapter 14)

WOOP. Gabriele Oettingen's evidence-based alternative to pure visualization: Wish (define the desire), Outcome (imagine the best result), Obstacle (identify the primary internal barrier), Plan (create an if-then strategy for the obstacle). Research shows this method outperforms positive visualization alone. (Chapter 1)

RESEARCH REFERENCES BY CHAPTER

Chapter 1: Desire

Oettingen, G. Rethinking Positive Thinking (2014). Gollwitzer, P. Implementation Intentions (1999). Huberman, A. Huberman Lab Podcast, episodes on dopamine and motivation.

Chapter 2: Faith

Bandura, A. Self-Efficacy: The Exercise of Control (1997). Dweck, C. Mindset: The New Psychology of Success (2006). Dunning, D. and Kruger, J. Unskilled and Unaware of It (1999). Sincero, J. You Are a Badass at Making Money (2017).

Chapter 3: Autosuggestion

Wood, J. et al. Positive Self-Statements, Psychological Science (2009). Doidge, N. The Brain That Changes Itself (2007). Kross, E. Chatter (2021). Clear, J. Atomic Habits (2018). Fogg, BJ. Tiny Habits (2019). Eker, T.H. Secrets of the Millionaire Mind (2005).

Chapter 4: Specialized Knowledge

Ericsson, A. Peak: Secrets from the New Science of Expertise (2016). Newport, C. Deep Work (2016). Adams, S. How to Fail at Almost Everything and Still Win Big (2013).

Chapter 5: Imagination

Koestler, A. The Act of Creation (1964). Amabile, T. Creativity in Context (1996). Land, G. and Jarman, B. Breakpoint and Beyond (1992). Wattles, W. The Science of Getting Rich (1910).

Chapter 6: Organized Planning

Adams, S. How to Fail at Almost Everything and Still Win Big (2013). Clear, J. Atomic Habits (2018). Doerr, J. Measure What Matters (2018). Ries, E. The Lean Startup (2011). Klein, G. Sources of Power (1998). DeMarco, MJ. The Millionaire Fastlane (2011). Ferriss, T. The 4-Hour Workweek (2007).

Chapter 7: Decision

Baumeister, R. Willpower (2011). Schwartz, B. The Paradox of Choice (2004). Levitt, S. Heads or Tails: The Impact of a Coin Toss, NBER (2020). Boyd, J. Patterns of Conflict (1986). Ferriss, T. The 4-Hour Workweek (2007).

Chapter 8: Persistence

Duckworth, A. Grit: The Power of Passion and Perseverance (2016). Duke, A. Quit: The Power of Knowing When to Walk Away (2022). Clear, J. Atomic Habits (2018).

Chapter 9: The Wealth Bridge

Housel, M. The Psychology of Money (2020). Kahneman, D. and Deaton, A. High Income Improves Evaluation of Life (2010). Killingsworth, M. Experienced Well-Being Rises with Income

(2021). Robin, V. Your Money or Your Life (1992). Ferriss, T. The 4-Hour Workweek (2007).

Chapter 10: The Master Mind

Granovetter, M. The Strength of Weak Ties (1973). Grant, A. Give and Take (2013). Putnam, R. Bowling Alone (2000).

Chapter 11: Energy Management

Csikszentmihalyi, M. Flow (1990). Walker, M. Why We Sleep (2017). Kleitman, N. Sleep and Wakefulness (1963). Ratey, J. Spark (2008). Lembke, A. Dopamine Nation (2021).

Chapter 12: The Mind-Brain Advantage

Kahneman, D., Thinking, Fast and Slow (2011); Munger, C., Poor Charlie's Almanack (2005); Parrish, S., Clear Thinking (2023); Eker, T.H., Secrets of the Millionaire Mind (2005); Doidge, N., The Brain That Changes Itself (2007); Harris, T., Center for Humane Technology research; Lembke, A., Dopamine Nation (2021); Allen, J., As a Man Thinketh (1903).

Chapter 13: The Sixth Sense

Klein, G. Sources of Power (1998). Kahneman, D. and Klein, G. Conditions for Intuitive Expertise (2009). Gigerenzer, G. Risk Savvy (2014). Gladwell, M. Blink (2005).

Chapter 14: The Modern Wealth Stack

Kiyosaki, R. Rich Dad Poor Dad (1997). DeMarco, MJ. The Millionaire Fastlane (2011). Bogle, J. The Little Book of Common Sense Investing (2007). Barber, B. and Odean, T. Trading Is Hazardous to Your Wealth (2000).

Chapter 15: The Anti-Guru

No formal academic sources. This chapter draws on the author's analysis of the financial advice industry's business models, incentive structures, and content strategies.

ACKNOWLEDGMENTS

This book exists because of the researchers whose work gave me something better than opinions: evidence. Daniel Kahneman, Angela Duckworth, James Clear, Carol Dweck, Gabriele Oettingen, Albert Bandura, Mihaly Csikszentmihalyi, Matthew Walker, Anna Lembke, Gary Klein, Gerd Gigerenzer, Charlie Munger, Shane Parrish, Norman Doidge, Cal Newport, BJ Fogg, Ethan Kross, Annie Duke, Adam Grant, Mark Granovetter, Barry Schwartz, and dozens of others. Any errors in translation are mine. The brilliance is theirs.

To Napoleon Hill, who started this conversation 90 years ago. I've spent this entire book lovingly disagreeing with you, which is the highest compliment one author can pay another. To Kiyosaki, DeMarco, Ferriss, Eker, Wattles, Allen, and Sincero: I borrowed your best ideas, credited them honestly, and tried to build something that honors the originals while fixing the parts that needed fixing.

A note of gratitude from Ken to Ibrahim: I have been in the creative trenches with you on more projects than either of us can count, and you brought your full instincts to this one too. Thank you for arguing every paragraph until it earned its place.

To Izzy, who builds things with her hands every day and who, over a kitchen table on a Sunday afternoon, gave me the most valuable financial insight of my life in one sentence: "I don't need more work. I need the right amount of the right work."

To every reader who picked up this book because they were tired of being sold to. I hope I've earned your trust.

And to the person reading this right now who is about to close this book and actually go build something: you're my favorite kind of reader. **Go.**

ABOUT THE AUTHORS

Ken Konet, M.Ed., MBA is a corporate instructional designer, behavioral science translator, and writer who has spent over two decades studying the gap between what people know and what they actually do. With three master's degrees and a career spanning education, corporate training, and independent publishing, he specializes in turning research into systems that change real-world behavior.

His professional work focuses on designing learning experiences that stick: training programs built on cognitive psychology, behavioral economics, and the science of habit formation. His writing applies the same principles to personal finance, self-development, and the art of thinking clearly in an age designed to prevent it.

He is the author of *Stop Stepping on Rakes, Adults Don't Exist, The Happiness Algorithm, Gamify Your Life for Success, The Discomfort Dividend, The Whole Child, Nobody Reads Your Resume at Your Funeral, Still Useful in an AI World, Migraines Demystified,* and *The Power of One*, among others. He has published across nonfiction, fiction, and children's genres.

He lives in Florida with his wife Izzy, a professional handywoman who is the most practically intelligent person he has ever met. He enjoys motorcycles, hiking, camping, and explaining cognitive biases to people who did not ask.

Ibrahim Roble is a writer and creative collaborator whose work spans literary horror, dark fantasy, psychological thriller, surreal fiction, and reimagined children's mythology. He has co-authored numerous fiction projects across multiple series, including *The Lucifera Series*, the *Monsterific* series, *The Harper Sisters*, and the standalone heist novel *Dream Heist*. His collaborations are unified by a recurring fascination with the moral architecture beneath genre conventions: how horror reveals what we fear about ourselves, how thriller exposes the patterns of predation hiding in plain sight, and how the strangest stories often carry the most honest lessons.

Think Again Loop is his first major nonfiction collaboration. He brings to it the same instinct for narrative architecture and human truth that shapes his fiction work, along with a co-author's willingness to argue every paragraph until it earned its place.

humbolton.com

Other Books from Humbolton Press

Ken Konet *Nonfiction, motivation, and instructional design*

Adults Don't Exist: Why No One Knows What They're Doing, and How to Think Anyway

The Discomfort Dividend: Why the Smartest Thing You Can Do as You Age Is Stop Running from What Hurts

The Engaged Leader: How to Build Trust, Empower Teams, and Lead with Impact

Gamify Your Life for Success: Level Up Your Goals, Habits, and Mindset

The Happiness Algorithm: How to Stop Chasing, Start Living, and Finally Take Control of Your Life

Migraines Demystified: Your Snarky, Science-Backed Survival Guide (with Elliott James)

Move Forward: Building Healthy Habits for a Fulfilling Life

Nobody Reads Your Resume at Your Funeral: Why What You're Tracking Isn't What Matters

The Power of One: One Word, One Habit, One Life (The Four Pillars of Power)

Still Useful in an AI World: The Human Playbook for the Age of AGI

Stop Stepping on Rakes: Laugh at Your Mistakes, Learn from Them, and Keep Moving Forward

The Whole Child: Raising Emotionally Intelligent Kids in a World That Forgot How

Happy Halloween: Hallowsville's Heroes (Hollowsville's Secrets, for younger readers)

Ken Konet & Ibrahim Roble *Fiction across horror, fantasy, thriller, and dark whimsy*

Accidental Assassin (The Harper Sisters, Book One)

Curb Appeal: A Forgotten Object. A Buried Network. A Deadly Trash Picking Mistake.

Demon Trainer: Exiled by Light, Forged in Flame

Dream Heist (The Reverie Heist)

Lucifera: The Anomoly (The Lucifera Series)

The Meaning of YOUR Life: Build a Life That Matters at Any Age, Any Stage

Mercy is Blind (The Lucifera Series, Book Two)

Midnight's Puppet: The Puppet that Shouldn't Smile (Monsterific Series)

The Shutoff

Winnie the Pooh and the Vampire: A Very Bitey Problem

Winnie the Pooh and The Zombies: A Rather Moaning Apocalypse

Heather Hollis *Literary fiction*

Sonnet 155: The Velvet Tongue

John & Sarah Pinkerton *The Pinkerton Papers, lifestyle and adult relationship guides*

Permission Granted: An Honest Field Guide to Bisexuality, Kink, and the Curious Middle

Chemistry of Kink: Why It Lights Us Up and What That Tells Us About Ourselves

Jordan Wright *Psychological thriller*

Mayor Mayhem: She Ran for Office and Took Out Corruption with a Safe Word (with Ibrahim Roble)

The Spider's Web: A Predator's Blueprint

Paul Green *Social commentary and cultural critique*

Bullies Run the World: A Survival Manual for Decent People Who Are Tired of Getting Worked

Same Slaves, Different Outfits: The Medieval Economy Hiding Inside Your 401(k) (with Andru Hale)

Stop Being Played: How Ignorance Hijacked Progress, and How We Get It Back (with Ibrahim Roble)

The Wealth Delusion: How Money and Power Distort the Mind

* * *

Humbolton Press is an independent publisher of nonfiction, fiction, and children's books that aim to be honest, useful, and worth the reader's time. Catalog and forthcoming titles at humbolton.com.

www.ingramcontent.com/pod-product-compliance
Lightning Source LLC
LaVergne TN
LVHW030910080826
845145LV00010B/2847

* 9 7 8 1 9 6 6 7 0 3 3 9 6 *